Reading with the Heart:
The Way into Narnia

Reading with the Heart: The Way into Narnia

by
Peter J. Schakel

WILLIAM B. EERDMANS PUBLISHING COMPANY
GRAND RAPIDS, MICHIGAN

Copyright© 1979 by Wm. B. Eerdmans Publishing Co.
255 Jefferson Ave. S.E., Grand Rapids, Mich. 49503
All rights reserved
Printed in the United States of America

Library of Congress Cataloging in Publication Data

Schakel, Peter J.
  Reading with the heart.

  Includes bibliographical references and index.
  1. Lewis, Clive Staples, 1898-1963. The chronicles of Narnia.
2. Fantastic fiction, English—History and criticism. I. Title.
PR6023.E926C538   823'.9'12   79-16471
ISBN 0-8028-1814-5

To Jennifer and Jonathan

Contents

Acknowledgments

*T*HE writing of this study was supported in part by a Mellon Faculty Development Grant from Hope College, for which I am very grateful. I am grateful also to Charles A. Huttar, Leland Ryken, and my wife Karen, for reading the manuscript and offering many helpful suggestions; to Greta Hutchins, who typed early drafts of several chapters, fitting them into an already crowded secretarial schedule; and to Phyllis Vandervelde, for her prompt and careful typing of the final draft. The staff of the Marion E. Wade Collection at Wheaton College provided willing and courteous assistance on several occasions. Although I owe a general debt to my students, both at Hope College and in several area churches, for their questions and comments regarding the Chronicles, I am particularly indebted, for ideas and the structure of Chapter 6, to a paper on *The Horse and His Boy* by Marilyn Pool.

Editions Used

O F the nearly ten million copies of the Narnia volumes that have been sold to date, about three-fourths have been in the Macmillan paperback edition. That edition seemed, therefore, the most convenient for the greatest number of readers as the source of quotations in this book.

The Lion, the Witch and the Wardrobe (1950; rpt. New York: Collier Books, 1970)

Prince Caspian: The Return to Narnia (1951; rpt. New York: Collier Books, 1970)

The Voyage of the "Dawn Treader" (1952; rpt. New York: Collier Books, 1970)

The Silver Chair (1953; rpt. New York: Collier Books, 1970)

The Horse and His Boy (1954; rpt. New York: Collier Books, 1970)

The Magician's Nephew (1955; rpt. New York: Collier Books, 1970)

The Last Battle (1956; rpt. New York: Collier Books, 1970)

Likewise I have used the Macmillan paperback edition of *Mere Christianity* (1952; reprinted New York: Macmillan,

1960). Page references for these books are included within parentheses in the text. For readers who wish to locate quotations in other editions, a table for converting page references to chapter numbers is provided at p. 148. References to all other books by Lewis are to the first edition.

Introduction

THE Chronicles of Narnia are, at present, the best-known and most influential works of a well-known and very influential writer. They outsell the rest of C. S. Lewis's works combined, at a rate now of several hundred thousand volumes per year. Regarded as classics by many authorities on children's literature, they are read and loved also by college students and older adults. And their popularity is probably not just a passing thing. "If asked which of Lewis's books I thought most likely to become immortals," Walter Hooper wrote a few years ago, "I should say the 'Narnian Chronicles.' "[1] Despite their sales and popularity, however, there seems to be a good deal of uncertainty about how the books should be read and understood—it is reflected in the questions some people raise about the books and in the articles other people write in reply.

Such uncertainty appears most directly in the question frequently asked about details in the Chronicles, "What does this stand for?" That the question is asked indicates that the Chronciles are not being approached as *stories* which are complete in themselves, but as works dependent on outside information for full meaning. Some people, therefore, refer to the stories as "allegories." If they mean by "allegory" only that the stories have more than one level of meaning, a religious significance beyond their plots, one cannot object: the tales do have theme, and sometimes several themes. If in referring to the Chronicles, however, they use "allegory" to mean an "extended metaphor in which objects, persons, and actions in a narrative . . . are equated with meanings that lie outside the narrative itself,"[2] to mean, in other words, that the reader is always to be asking what this or that "symbolizes," then I at least must demur. To view them so misses Lewis's main intent and runs the danger of distorting their artistry and detracting from their universal meanings as fairy tales.

In the essays which follow, I will give a reading of the Chronicles which, I believe, clarifies and enhances their intent and techniques, while avoiding the problems an "allegorical" approach raises. I will outline and then apply to the Chronicles a critical approach consistent with Lewis's ideas about "pure story."[3] I will suggest that Lewis created in his stories "secondary worlds" which he expected readers to enter imaginatively and to respond to, initially, with their hearts rather than with their heads. For such an approach, the sources of Lewis's ideas, the influences upon his techniques, the history of the forms in which he worked, and the similarities of his other works to the Chronicles are of little importance. The emphasis will be on the stories themselves, starting with what Lewis once called "the genuinely critical question 'Why, and how, should we read this?' "[4] For that reason I do not, for the most part, include explanatory references from other essays or books by Lewis: they should not be needed and might encourage readers to intellectualize the Chronicles, rather than enter them imaginatively.

There is one major exception to that, however. I have referred frequently to *Mere Christianity*, not because its explanations are necessary to make Narnia meaningful, but because of what seems to me a special imaginative relationship between it and the images and stories of Narnia. *Mere Christianity* was published in 1952. At some point during the time he was writing the Chronicles (between 1949 and 1953) Lewis revised the three separate volumes of BBC talks into a single volume, making additions and deletions, rephrasing sentences, expanding the contractions, and eliminating the use of italics for emphasis.[5] Thus, *Mere Christianity* was fresh in Lewis's mind during the period in which he was writing the Chronicles and that might account, in part at least, for the numerous parallels in imagery and word choice between it and various Chronicles. Those parallels, in several instances, seem to be central to the plot or structure of the stories and to have a significance far beyond clarification of a particular idea or doctrine in the stories.

For a similar reason I have rarely used Bible texts to illustrate or clarify meanings in the story.[6] To look for biblical parallels or illustrations implies that the Chronicles are dependent on biblical glosses for fullest clarity and effectiveness, rather than being self-sufficient and containing their own meanings. And only rarely, when they are of special importance, have I pointed out biblical allusions, or brief, passing verbal echoings of the Bible. At times readers who know the Bible well will find phrases or situations in the Chronicles which remind them of biblical phrases or situations. Such reminders are natural and to be expected: they are part of the ripple effect within the whole of literature. But the recognition of the allusions should be almost automatic, a tidbit which enriches the experience for the reader alert or knowledgeable enough to notice. The effect is spoiled if the allusion must be pointed out and explained. For me to mention them regularly might suggest that the books are meant especially for the informed, for those who recognize such references. That, I firmly believe, is not the case.

The key to the approach of this book, then, is that it assumes the Chronicles are not dependent on works or ideas outside themselves, either through allegory or allusion. They depict secondary worlds, separate and self-contained, and they are to be "received" as such, through the imagination and the emotions. My goal in this study, therefore, is to send readers back to the Chronicles with interest renewed and enjoyment increased; to bring out the universal character of the stories by focusing on archetypal motifs, characters, and images; and to clarify the broad patterns of Christian meaning—not picky parallels—which Lewis develops within the books.

1

Reading with the Heart: The Critical Approach

*I*N beginning a chapter late in *Mere Christianity* Lewis wrote, "It is a very silly idea that in reading a book you must never 'skip.' All sensible people skip freely when they come to a chapter which they find is going to be no use to them. In this chapter I am going to talk about something which may be helpful to some readers, but which may seem to others merely an unnecessary complication. If you are one of the second sort of readers, then I advise you not to bother about this chapter at all but to turn on to the next" (p. 145). Readers should approach the first chapter of this book, too, with that attitude. This chapter shows how an understanding of and attention to the form, archetypes, narrative category, and conventions of a work can make one a more skillful reader, able to respond more fully to a work of fiction. Readers who find this chapter uninteresting or bewildering should go on to the next one, and, perhaps, return to it after reading the chapters which follow.

In *A Preface to Paradise Lost* Lewis asserts that "the first qualification for judging any piece of workmanship from a corkscrew to a cathedral is to know *what* it is— what it was intended to do and how it is meant to be used."[1] As we consider the question of how the Chronicles of Nar-

1

nia should be read, we must begin by giving attention to their form, to the kind of literature they are. Lewis himself called them fairy tales and, more specifically, the type of fairy tales known as fantasies.[2] Fairy tales, by definition, are short stories involving supernatural events and characters such as elves, fairy godmothers, and witches, set in whole or in part in a never-never land.[3] Lewis's friend, J. R. R. Tolkien, whose ideas influenced Lewis greatly, defines a "fairy-story" as "one which touches on or uses Faërie, whatever its own main purpose may be: satire, adventure, morality, fantasy."[4] "Faërie itself," Tolkien goes on to say, "may perhaps most nearly be translated by Magic—but it is magic of a peculiar mood and power," the power of Enchantment.[5] As fairy tales, then, the Chronicles will be characterized by strangeness and wonder, usually produced by magic, but at the same time, as fantasies, they must be believable and have internal consistency. Such believability is attained, in fairy tales which are also fantasies, by creation of a separate, "enchanted" world into which characters and readers are taken.

A fantasy, in literary terms, is "a work which takes place in a non-existent and unreal world, such as fairyland."[6] A fantasy world should be independent of our world and self-sufficient: all the information needed to understand actions and meanings should be available within that world. It is an imaginary world and may have natural laws different from those of our world, but once those laws are established, they must be adhered to—if they are ignored or violated, the magic spell of the story will be broken. Tolkien again provides a useful explanation: "What really happens is that the story-maker proves a successful 'sub-creator.' He makes a Secondary World which your mind can enter. Inside it, what he relates is 'true': it accords with the laws of that world. You therefore believe it, while you are, as it were, inside."[7] George MacDonald, the Scottish preacher and story writer whom Lewis called his "teacher," offers a similar account: "Man may, if he pleases, invent a little world of his own, with its own laws; for there is that in him which delights in calling up new forms— which is the nearest, perhaps, he can come to creation. . . . His world once invented, the highest law that comes next into play is, that there shall be harmony between the laws by which the new world has begun to exist; and in the process of his creation, the inventor must hold by those laws. The moment he forgets one of them, he makes the story, by its own postulates, incredible."[8] It is such a "secondary" or "suppositional" world that Lewis creates in Narnia. As we enter Narnia we encounter an imaginary world in which animals can talk, in which creatures mythical in our world are real, and in which creatures unknown in our world have an important place. And as we pass through the wardrobe into that world, we must accept it as real, we must embrace it imaginatively and yield ourselves to it so long as the story lasts.

From the first, however, there has been a tendency to neglect the form of the Chronicles and to stress methods of reading which subvert the effects a fantasy seeks to attain. That has been the result many times when the Chronicles are treated as "allegories," works whose events and characters must "stand for" or point to things outside their fictional world in order to be understood or appreciated fully. A review of *The Last Battle* in the *Times Literary Supplement* (11 May 1956) noted that "the conclusion is striking, and the allegory, for an adult at least, is clear." In the first study of the series as a whole, an otherwise sensitive and helpful essay, Charles A. Brady wrote, "Allegory is strong in Narnia."[9] And more recently John W. Montgomery held that "the Narnia Chronicles contain powerful and deep Christian allegory woven into their very fiber."[10] To take the Chronicles as allegory, however, raises the danger of breaking their spell, either by destroying the independence of the imaginary world, as we begin looking outside it for the completion of its meaning, or by leading us to use our heads rather than our hearts in responding to the stories, or both. There are passages in the Chronicles which allow allegorical readings: Aslan's death in *The Lion, the Witch and the Wardrobe,* Eustace's transformation in Aslan's well in *The Voyage of the "Dawn Treader,"* and the final judgment and destruction of the world in *The Last Battle,* for example, have close parallels in Christianity and their meaning inevitably will be shaped to some extent by those parallels. But a brief comment by MacDonald puts them into proper perspective: "A fairytale is not an allegory. There may be allegory in it, but it is not an allegory."[11] Unfortunately a few such passages, especially in *The Lion, the Witch and the Wardrobe,* have exerted undue influence and have led some readers to look for parallels everywhere and to ask what every large or small detail is supposed to symbolize.

More typical of Lewis's technique in the Chronicles than those passages is a use of narrative which, as is common in fairy tales, borders on or passes completely into the realm of myth. Lewis, like most students of literature, rarely uses myth in its familiar sense of a "fictitious story, or unscientific account, theory, belief, etc." Generally he uses it in a positive sense and it becomes a vital element in his thought. A myth, according to Lewis, is a narrative with a simple, satisfactory and inevitable shape which imparts to its readers' imaginations a real though unfocused gleam of divine truth.[12] A myth, in other words, is a story, a narrative; it depends for effect upon its shape, upon what happens to whom for what reasons, not upon the particular words or style in which it is told; it must communicate imaginatively, not intellectually; and at its heart must be a truth of universal significance or applicability. Lewis believed that allegory and myth can be placed on a sort of continuum: "When allegory is at its best, it approaches myth, which must be grasped with the imagination, not with the intellect."[13] When allegory is at its best, at its most imaginative, and when myth is least effective, most nearly intellectual, they are close to each other. But from that meeting point at the center, they move by their natures in opposite directions, toward the intellectual and the imaginative, respectively. Here perhaps is the best resolution to the debate over "allegory" in the Chronicles. At their very best, as for example in the final pages of *The Voyage of the "Dawn Treader"* and the final chapter of *The Last Battle,* the Chronicles are high myth, communicating so directly to the imagination and emotions through powerful images and symbols that they cannot be translated fully into intellectual terms. Occasionally, where passages suggest a single meaning apprehended by the intellect through reference to the Bible or Christianity, they move into the allegorical half of the spectrum. Most of the time, however, they lie slightly to the myth side of the dividing line, so that their primary and most profitable appeal is to the imagination, not to the intellect.

So, apparently, Lewis himself thought it should be. He tried to set matters straight in his essay "Sometimes Fairy Stories May Say Best What's to be Said": "Some people seem to think that I began by asking myself how I could say something about Christianity to children; then fixed on the fairy tale as an instrument; then . . . drew up a list of basic Christian truths and hammered out 'allegories' to embody them. This is all pure moonshine. I couldn't write in that way at all" *(Of Other Worlds,* p. 36). Elsewhere he cites the use of a secondary world as evidence that Aslan is not to be taken as an allegorical figure:

> In reality . . . he is an invention giving an imaginary answer to the question, "What might Christ become like, if there really were a world like Narnia and He chose to be incarnate and die and rise again in *that* world as He actually has done in ours?" This is not allegory at all. . . . The Incarnation of Christ in another world is mere supposal; but *granted* the

supposition, He would really have been a physical object in that world as He was in Palestine.[14]

Lewis expected his readers to enter his supposed world fully, to accept it as real and self-contained, and not to be asking what details in Narnia stand for in our world or looking for meanings that can be abstracted from the story through allegory. Their primary appeal, he expected, would be to the heart, not the head. George MacDonald summarizes it all by comparing the fairy tale to music, and Lewis surely would agree with him: "The best way with music, I imagine, is not to bring the forces of our intellect to bear upon it, but to be still and let it work on that part of us for whose sake it exists. We spoil countless precious things by intellectual greed. . . . If any strain of my 'broken music' make a child's eyes flash, or his mother's grow for a moment dim, my labour will not have been in vain."[15]

But there are echoes in the Chronicles; there are events and characters and phrases which remind one of the Bible, or the classics, or other fairy tales. Lewis would say, however, as a more recent literary theorist has also, that these are examples of archetype, not of allegory. And a second step toward answering the question "How should the Chronicles of Narnia be read?" involves coming to grips with the term "archetype." Formidable as the word sounds, its dictionary meaning is simply a model, an example of a type or group. The literary scholar uses "archetype" more specifically as a symbol, character type, or plot motif that has recurred throughout literature.[16] Writers in all ages have used gardens, calm, festivity, and harvest, for example, as symbols of desirable states of being and deserts, storms, discord, and drought as corresponding symbols of undesirable conditions; and they have used the hero, the benevolent king, and the wise older guide as good characters, while the villain, the tyrant, and the witch appear

again and again as the corresponding evil figure. Throughout the centuries writer after writer, similarly, has in-
voked such motifs as the quest, the journey into experience,
and the Cinderella pattern in developing the plot of his or
her story. Each use of such a typical or recurring symbol,
character type, or plot motif, in Northrop Frye's words,
"connects one poem with another and thereby helps to unify
and integrate our literary experience."[17] The examples
listed above, therefore, all taken from the Chronicles, con-
nect Lewis's tales with the long literary tradition that preceded them.

Among the most used and most important of such archetypal images are the seasonal cycle of spring, summer,
autumn, and winter, the daily cycle of dawn, zenith, sunset, and night, and the life cycle of youth, adulthood, old
age, and death. Throughout history poets have seen analogies among these natural cycles; the relations between
them might be illustrated on a simple diagram:

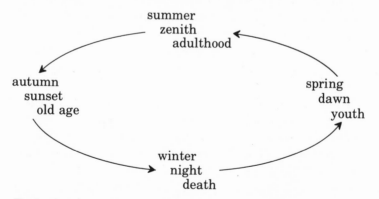

Each time we speak of the "sunset" or "golden" years of
life in referring to old age, or describe death as being "sleep,"
we are, consciously or unconsciously, invoking those archetypes. And the Chronicles, as fairy tales dealing with basic
stories and themes, use those cycles in several ways. The
seasonal cycle is used, for example, in *The Lion, the Witch*

and the Wardrobe as the children "saw the winter vanishing and the whole wood passing in a few hours or so from January to May" (p. 120). The daily cycle of the sun becomes an important element in *The Horse and His Boy* as the two children and two horses undertake a journey into experience across the desert. Even Narnia comes full circle, from its origin in *The Magician's Nephew* to its ending—and continuation in another world—in *The Last Battle*.

Beyond the meaning of the individual cycles is the significance of the patterns as a whole. "In the solar cycle of the day," Frye explains, "the seasonal cycle of the year, and the organic cycle of human life, there is a single pattern of significance"; elsewhere he calls that pattern the "story of the loss and regaining of identity," which is "the framework of all literature," the single story or "monomyth" underlying it all.[18] The story of Prince Rilian, as he loses and regains his identity in *The Silver Chair,* illustrates that theme nicely, as does the trilogy of books— *Prince Caspian, The Voyage of the "Dawn Treader,"* and *The Silver Chair*—which follows Caspian through youth, maturing, old age, death, and resurrection. But one could go further and show quite readily that the problem of identity—of learning who one is and maturing in that knowledge—is present in each of the Chronicles. Here once again we see the interconnectedness of literature, and the close relationship between literature and life. "Putting works of literature in such a context gives them an immense reverberating dimension of significance . . . , in which every literary work catches the echoes of all other works of its type in literature, and so ripples out into the rest of literature and thence into life" (Frye, *Fables of Identity,* p. 37).

The Chronicles have their roots in many other stories, in the fairy tales and myths of the past. Recognition and consideration of several features as archetypes drawn from those roots is very helpful in reading the Chronicles. It allows a reader, for example, to see the death and return to life of Aslan in the first book as an archetypal motif, part of the pattern Lewis refers to in *Mere Christianity* as the "good dreams" God sent the human race: "I mean those queer stories scattered all through the heathen religions about a god who dies and comes to life again and, by his death, has somehow given new life to men" (p. 54). The death of Aslan in Narnia has additional vibrations, a deeper and fuller meaning, because it fits into a pattern in nature and in literature (or mythology) that preceded it, including, of course, the death of Christ in our world, which was the greatest example of the archetype because it was historical fact as well as myth.[19]

Recognition of archetypes can also help avoid misreadings. The White Witch in *The Lion, the Witch and the Wardrobe,* for example, has often been allegorized as the Devil of our world.[20] But the Witch is not the Devil. The details of the story make that clear. She is of human ancestry—a descendant of Adam's first wife, Lilith[21]—and she is mortal: the story says definitely that she dies at the end of the battle.[22] She is, of course, the evil force in the traditional fairy-tale separation of good from evil; but to conclude that she is, therefore, the Devil is to read with the head rather than the heart. She is simply the archetypal figure of the temptress witch, whom we respond to quite directly as "bad." And that is how Lewis himself viewed her: "The Witch," he wrote in a letter, "is of course Circe, . . . because she is . . . the same Archtype we find in so many fairy tales. No good asking where any individual author got *that*. We are born knowing the Witch, aren't we?"[23] Circe, in the *Odyssey,* tempted men with magical food and turned them into animals. The Witch, by her affinities with Circe, fits the same pattern, or archetype, as the witch who caught Hansel and Gretel, the old witch in Grimm's "Sweetheart Roland," and the Wicked Witch of the West in *The Wizard of Oz:* each tempts its prey, hates human beings, and epitomizes selfishness, cruelty, and desire for control. Each suggests to children the nature of evil, but is not herself an embodiment or symbol of the Devil. Lewis seems to have intended that the White Witch be paired (since "every typical character in romance tends to have his moral opposite confronting him"—Frye, *Anatomy of Criticism*, p. 195) with Father Christmas, rather than with Aslan. The Witch is white, cold, greedy, and cruel, in contrast to the red colors, warmth, generosity, and kindliness of the traditional patron figure of Christmas.[24] In his use of archetypes, too, Lewis expects his readers to remain, for the most part, within the work. Archetypes are not allegories, pointing outside themselves to the meaning that completes them. Rather they embody within themselves the tradition they represent and the significance they have accumulated over the years. They also are to be approached not with the acumen of the head but with the sensitivity and receptivity of the heart.

The question of how to read the Chronicles leads next to two characteristics which further shape our imaginative and emotional reaction to the stories, their *mythoi* and their use of conventions. First, as one reads a work of fiction, Frye emphasizes, one must be sensitive to its narrative type, what he calls its *mythos* (*Anatomy of Criticism*, pp. 158-62). The *mythos*, for Frye, is a broad "narrative category," not the embodiment of that category in a specific form or genre; it is the general model which clarifies to us how we are to react to the plot of a work, whatever its genre, or class, may be. "If we are told that what we are about to read is tragic or comic, we expect a certain kind of structure and mood, but not necessarily a certain genre" (*Anatomy of Criticism*, p. 162). The combination of structure and mood is its *mythos*, and one must give attention to it as one reads in order to know how to respond—whether to take difficulties seriously (in a tragic work) or lightly (in a comic work). If we do not notice the cues, or if we encounter a work (such as dark comedy) where the signals are not typical, we can find ourselves confused and uncertain as we read. There are four *mythoi*—tragedy, comedy, romance, and irony—and, in a major critical innovation, Frye aligns each with the segment of the natural cycles whose imagery usually appears in, or characterizes, that *mythos*. Thus he links spring with comedy, summer with romance, autumn with tragedy, and winter with irony or antiromance. The common structures of myths, he concludes, which were based on the cycles of nature, became in due course the structural principles of literature:

> The absorption of the natural cycle into mythology provides myth with two of these structures; the rising movement that we find in myths of spring or the dawn, of birth, marriage and resurrection, and the falling movement in myths of death, metamorphosis, or sacrifice. These movements reappear as the structural principles of comedy and tragedy in literature. Again, the dialectic in myth that projects a paradise or heaven above our world and a hell or place of shades below it reappears in literature as the idealized world of pastoral and romance and the absurd, suffering, or frustrated world of irony and satire. *(Fables of Identity,* pp. 33-34)

In the case of the Chronicles of Narnia, one must begin with the understanding that, within their form as fairy tales, they employ the narrative pattern, or *mythos,* of romance. The romance is characterized by a standard plot, one of quest or adventure, often undertaken by a single knight; it is set in a courtly and chivalric age, often one of highly developed manners and chivalry; it stresses knightly ideals of courage, honor, mercifulness to an opponent; it usually introduces a heroine, and frequently its central interest is romantic love, together with tournaments fought and dragons slain for a damsel's sake; and it delights in wonders and marvels, making much of the mysterious effect of magic, spells, and enchantments.[25] "The mode of romance," as Frye sums it up, "presents an idealized world:

11

... heroes are brave, heroines beautiful, villains villain-ous, and the frustrations, ambiguities, and embarrass-ments of ordinary life are made little of" *(Anatomy of Criticism,* p. 151).

By combining the narrative pattern of romance with the structural form of the fairy tale, Lewis was able to adapt the latter to his specific needs in the Chronicles. The fairy-tale form, he wrote in "Sometimes Fairy Stories May Say Best What's to be Said," allowed him to eliminate the traditional love interest of the romance and to avoid its tendency toward elevated language: "As these images sorted themselves into events (i.e., became a story) they seemed to demand no love interest and no close psychology. But the Form which excludes these things is the fairy tale. And the moment I thought of that I fell in love with the Form itself: its brevity, its severe restraints on description. ... Its very limitations of vocabulary became an attrac-tion" *(Of Other Worlds,* pp. 36-37). And it allowed him to give to exciting action, even to violence—removed from the real world by the double cushions of the fairy tale and the romance mode—the positive values of the chivalric age Lewis loved. There is no use hiding from children, Lewis asserted in "On Three Ways of Writing for Children," that they are "born into a world of death, violence, wounds, adventure, heroism and cowardice, good and evil." For that reason Lewis does not share the reservations some feel about having such matters in children's stories: "I side im-penitently with the human race against the modern re-former. Let there be wicked kings and beheadings, battles and dungeons, giants and dragons, and let villains be soundly killed at the end of the book" *(Of Other Worlds,* p. 31). Combining the fairy tale with the romance joins the primitive perspectives of the former with the positive, idealistic outlook of the latter to create an appeal for chil-dren and adults alike.

One must be alert to a work's *mythos* in order to know

how to respond to it, but also in order to be aware of its use of, and departures from, the conventions of its type. Each *mythos* has over the centuries developed a set of conventions, the "rules" by which the "game" of that type is played. Like the rules of a game, the conventions of a genre must be accepted if one is to enjoy a story as it is written. "The king's rash promise, the cuckold's jealousy, the 'lived happily ever after' tag to a concluding marriage, the manipulated happy endings of comedy in general . . . all exist solely as story-telling devices" *(Fables of Identity,* p. 36). To understand an author's work well, one must recognize where the work is following conventions and where it is departing from conventions. Departure from convention (Frye calls it "displacement"—adaptation or modification of narrative or thematic patterns to fit some standard of plausibility or morality) is particularly important because in it an author often reveals his or her individual intent or emphasis. The Chronicles of Narnia rely heavily on conventions: their importance is suggested in *The Lion, the Witch and the Wardrobe* when Edmund asks Peter if the robin they are following might be leading them into a trap. "That's a nasty idea," Peter replies. "Still—a robin you know. They're good birds in all the stories I've ever read. I'm sure a robin wouldn't be on the wrong side" (p. 59).

Recognizing conventions, particularly conventions borrowed from the romance tradition, can help prevent misreading or misunderstanding of the Chronicles. The Chronicles have been criticized, for example, as being racist, sexist, and overly violent.[26] To criticize Lewis fairly, however, one must consider the conventions of the *mythos* within which he was writing. One may well regret the emphasis on the dark skins and garlicy breath of the Calormenes and the dwarfs' references to the Calormenes as "Darkies." But the Calormenes are not simply "dark persons"—they are Moors: they are identified by their dress, weapons, and manners as the traditional enemy in medieval romances. More important, however, than Lewis's use of this convention are his frequent departures from and adaptations of it. The enemies in most of the books are not dark: the Telmarines in *Prince Caspian* are light-skinned and the Witch in *The Lion, the Witch and the Wardrobe* and *The Magician's Nephew* is white. Even more significantly, not all Calormenes are evil—a notable exception is Emeth in *The Last Battle*—and one even becomes queen of Archenland, when she marries the fair-skinned hero of *The Horse and His Boy*.

The stories do limit males and females to traditional roles more than today's consciousness-raised society prefers, particularly in *The Lion, the Witch and the Wardrobe*. Such stereotyping is conventional in romances, as women are routinely placed on pedestals, helpless in the face of dangers from which the dauntless heroes must rescue them; and such stereotyping, therefore, should be expected to some extent in the Chronicles. More important than the stereotypes, however, are the places where Lewis departs from convention. He frequently, and increasingly as the series proceeds, gives positions of leadership to girls: Lucy, for example, undertakes a challenging task in *The Voyage of the "Dawn Treader."* And Jill Pole, in *The Last Battle,* leads Tirian and Eustace through a dark forest to Stable Hill and participates in combat as an equal.

And there is violence in the Chronicles: it is part of the romance tradition Lewis was using. But there is less violence than one would expect if Lewis were closely following the romance convention, with its tendency toward sudden, barely motivated violence: three books, *The Voyage of the "Dawn Treader," The Silver Chair,* and *The Magician's Nephew,* contain very little violence at all. When violence does appear in the other books, it is used as a metaphor, as battles against evil, which is strong and aggressive and must be resisted actively. It is an old metaphor: "The idea of the knight—the Christian in arms for the defence of a good cause—is one of the great Christian ideas" *(Mere Christianity,* p. 107). But it is most significant that the Chronicles do not follow the typical romance in presenting strength as the way to solve problems. The good side in Narnia is always the weaker side, physically: Narnia itself is a tiny country, "not the fourth size of one of [the] least provinces" of the powerful nation of Calormen *(The Horse and His Boy,* p. 108). The Narnian forces usually consist, as they do in *Prince Caspian,* of "a handful of Dwarfs and woodland creatures" who wonder how they can "defeat an army of grown-up humans" (pp. 109-10). Victory for the Narnians comes only through Aslan: that, perhaps, is the central theme of the series. Awareness of the forms and conventions that lie behind the Chronicles, then, and of Lewis's departures from those conventions, is important to a full and accurate understanding of what the Chronicles are about.

Throughout this chapter we have been concerned with the question of how the Chronicles of Narnia should be read. We have given attention to several characteristics which can prevent misreading or misunderstanding them. In doing so, however, we have actually been answering a broader question, that of how stories in general should be read. All fiction creates an imaginary world, draws upon archetypes, and employs a *mythos* and conventions, and as we become alert to their importance and uses, we become equipped to read stories of various sorts. The question of how stories should be read is one that interested Lewis greatly. He dealt with it at some length in his essay "On Stories." All of what we have discussed here, along with such standard storytelling methods as contrast, foreshadowing, climax, and characterization, must come together into what Lewis calls the flavor or "quality" of the story, which must be tasted by the imagination and emotions of the reader. In "On Stories" Lewis complains that critics have paid too little attention to "Story considered in itself" *(Of Other Worlds,* p. 3). Critics seem to have assumed that books read merely "for the story" are read for the excitement they convey. Lewis tries to show that story can give another sort of pleasure, absorption into the "whole world" created by the story. Each story develops a distinctive image, or quality, or environment which determines the unique nature of the imaginative response it calls forth. "To be stories at all they must be series of events: but it must be understood that this series—the *plot,* as we call it—is only really a net whereby to catch something else. The real theme may be, and perhaps usually is, something that has no sequence in it, something other than a process and much more like a state or quality" *(Of Other Worlds,* p. 18). A story about danger from giants has a different quality from a story about danger from Indians, a story of isolation on the moon has a different quality from one about isolation in Siberia. Each has its own "idea," its own unique imaginative quality. That quality, which is not a fact, like death, but a state, like the sense of the deathly, gives books deeper and more lasting appeal than just excitement: it gives an imaginative and emotional pleasure which makes romances "a sort of poetry" for the uneducated reader *(Of Other Worlds,* p. 17). And that quality becomes, in a well-written work, the unifying factor of the work: "Every episode, every speech, helps to incarnate what the author is imagining. You could spare none of them. It takes the whole story to build [it] up" *(Of Other Worlds,* p. 19). Such a sense of unifying theme or "total design" should come through for each of the Chronicles of Narnia in the essays which follow.

An inevitable part of that "total design" for a person like Lewis is his religion. For someone with a Christian commitment as deep as Lewis's, faith has to affect the nature and quality of the stories he or she writes. Lewis said as much in his essay "On Three Ways of Writing for Children," although he uses the broader word "moral" in the essay. As you write, "let the pictures tell you their own moral. For the moral inherent in them will rise from whatever spiritual roots you have succeeded in striking during the whole course of your life" *(Of Other Worlds,* p. 33). That perhaps clarifies Lewis's own comments about the origins of the Chronicles in "Sometimes Fairy Stories May Say Best What's to be Said." "Everything began with images," he wrote; "a faun carrying an umbrella, a queen on a sledge, a magnificent lion. At first there wasn't even anything Christian about them." As he worked with those images, the qualities inherent in them asserted themselves: the Christian element "pushed itself in of its own accord" *(Of Other Worlds,* p. 36). To assert that the Chronicles are not allegories is not to play down the importance of Christianity in them. Rather, it is to suggest that the Christian meaning is deeper and more subtle than the term allegory permits, that, when the Chronicles are at their best, they do not just convey Christian meanings intellectually, by "representations," but they communicate directly to the imagination and the emotions a sizable share of the central elements of the Christian faith. But the meaning is not limited to the Christian aspects, as it would be in a representational method. The use of myth allows other meanings to ray out from the stories, enables the stories to say what the author "does not yet know and cd. not come by in any other way" *(Letters of C. S. Lewis,* p. 271).

In *An Experiment in Criticism* Lewis mentions that people read literature, as they approach the other arts, either to "use" it or to "receive" it. "A work of (whatever) art," he wrote, "can be either 'received' or 'used.' When we 'receive' it we exert our senses and imagination and various other powers according to a pattern invented by the artist. When we 'use' it we treat it as assistance for our own activities" (p. 88). There has been a tendency, or at least a temptation, among some readers to "use" the

Chronicles of Narnia, by considering them narrowly as devotional literature or by searching them for religious meanings of a limited and obvious sort. So long as the user avoids the danger of distortion, of imposing his or her own pattern on the work and thus finding what is not really there, "use" is a legitimate even if, as Lewis would say, an "inferior" activity *(An Experiment in Criticism,* p. 88). Better one should "use" literature, music, or art than not read, listen, or look at all. Better still, however, learn to "receive" the full pleasure and meaning that the work, through its shape and texture, can provide. That, in sum, is the intention of this book, to help people read the Chronicles first with their hearts, then with their heads, and always according to the pattern Lewis invented.

2

"A Great Sculptor's Shop": Law and Grace in *The Lion, the Witch and the Wardrobe*

"**A**LL my seven Narnian books," Lewis wrote in 1960, "and my three science fiction books, began with seeing pictures in my head. At first they were not a story, just pictures. The *Lion* all began with a picture of a Faun carrying an umbrella and parcels in a snowy wood." He decided one day to try to make a story out of that and a few other pictures, without knowing how or where the story would go. "But then suddenly Aslan came bounding into it" and gave direction and unity to the story: he drew the Christian element in and "pulled the whole story together."[1] Important as Aslan is, however, the unity of the story depends less upon him than upon magic, the quality which determines the imaginative response to the book and gives it a more complete unity than the unity of character. The flavor of magic permeates *The Lion, the Witch and the Wardrobe*, unifying event and image, technique and theme, atmosphere and archetype. Through it the finest effects of the story are achieved—the transformation of what are intellectual concepts in our world into images which affect readers imaginatively and emotionally in the world of Narnia.

The opening chapters of the book establish the basic

magic of Narnia. It is introduced by a magic wardrobe: in the words of Lucy, who entered it first, "It's—it's a magic wardrobe. There's a wood inside it, and it's snowing, and there's a Faun and a witch and it's called Narnia" (p. 21). The magic works next for Edmund, who follows Lucy through the wardrobe a few days later and encounters a different kind of magic: a great lady in white who produces a cup of hot drink and a box of enchanted Turkish Delight by dropping liquid into the snow. Later, by a still different magic all four children enter Narnia through the wardrobe. In order to keep out of the way of the housekeeper, Mrs. Macready, and a whole gang of sightseers, who seem to be coming wherever they go, the children enter the wardrobe room and then the wardrobe itself. It was as if "some magic in the house had come to life and was chasing them into Narnia" (p. 49). Lewis uses magic, then, as it was used in works of the Middle Ages which "have unmistakably the note of 'faerie' about them."[2] From the opening chapter, this note of magic, or enchantment, is vital to *The Lion, the Witch and the Wardrobe,* providing the basic characteristic of the world in which its action takes place.

There is also in these opening chapters what Tolkien calls the "elvish craft," the magic which "produces a Secondary World into which both designer and spectator can enter."[3] It is the magic of the storyteller, using narrative devices to enable the reader to accept and share the experiences of the Pevensie children as they enter Narnia. The vivid details allow the reader to participate with Lucy in the experience of encountering Narnia for the first time, as she reaches ahead into the darkness of the wardrobe, hears a crunching underfoot, feels the cold wetness of the snow and the prickliness of the trees, and glimpses the light of the lamp-post ahead of her. The reader shares her bewilderment and uncertainty about where she is and what she has gotten into. Lewis continues to make the world she has entered real and believable by the detailed descriptions of Tumnus's cave and tea (p. 13) and of his struggle over whether to reveal Lucy's identity: "The Faun's brown eyes had filled with tears and then the tears began trickling down his cheeks, and soon they were running off the end of his nose; and at last he covered his face with his hands and began to howl" (p. 14). He also makes the story convincing by the initial skepticism of the other children. The first to enter Narnia is the youngest and most impressionable. The older, clear-headed realists Edmund, Susan, and Peter are sure that there could not be, and that there is not, any such world through the wardrobe—until they get there. The empirical evidence of actually entering Narnia, which brushes aside their skepticism, convinces the skeptical reader as well.

Lewis also uses the standard devices of mystery and adventure to involve the reader in the action imaginatively and emotionally. The story holds one's interest by the aura of mystery (the rambling house and strange new land), by the questions that need answers (why is it always winter? who is Aslan?), and by the excitement of entering Narnia and braving the perils in it. The unifying adventure, finding and aiding Tumnus the Faun, contains both mystery and excitement. Having discovered that Tumnus is missing because of the help he gave Lucy, the children decide they "simply must try to rescue him" (p. 56), however dangerous that may be. And the reader follows that adventure with interest and uncertainty throughout the story.

Finally Lewis, from early in the story, begins to build in foreshadowings which set up later parts: that it is always winter anticipates the climax of the story as the warmth and joy of Christmas signal the end of the Witch's cold and selfish reign. Mention of "the four thrones at Cair Paravel" (p. 17) anticipates the conclusion of the book, as do the fur coats that looked "like royal robes" (p. 52) on the four children. All of these devices—of participation, mystery, and foreshadowing—are united in the first mention of Aslan:

> "They say Aslan is on the move—perhaps has already landed."
> And now a very curious thing happened. None of the children knew who Aslan was any more than you do; but the moment the Beaver had spoken these words everyone felt quite different. ... At the name of Aslan each one of the children felt something jump in his inside. (p. 64)

The reader, too, to some extent, shares the experience. He or she doesn't know who Aslan is, but some of the sense of excitement, of awe, and of expectation is conveyed to him or her as it is to the children.

The magic of Narnia and of the narrative is used to introduce, although it is apparent only in retrospect, the theme of Deep Magic, or the Law of Human Nature. The theme focuses on Edmund. After the four children have entered Narnia, discovered that Tumnus the Faun has been captured by the Witch for helping Lucy, and been informed and fed by Beaver and his wife, a crucial episode occurs. Edmund, still lusting for the White Witch's candy, commits the treasonous act of deserting his brother and sisters and betraying their plans to the Witch. Edmund's act violates the most basic demands of justice and fair play. Even the youngest of readers will recognize that Edmund has done a very basic and serious wrong. Edmund himself does not assert that what he did was right or good; he only attempts to justify it:

> But he managed to believe, or to pretend he believed, that [the Witch] wouldn't do anything very bad to [Peter, Susan, and Lucy], "Because," he said to himself, "all these people who say nasty things about her are her enemies and probably half of it isn't true. She was jolly nice to me, anyway, much nicer than they are. I expect she is the rightful Queen really. Anyway, she'll be better than that awful Aslan!" At least, that was the excuse he made in his own mind for what he

was doing. It wasn't a very good excuse, however, for deep down inside him he really knew that the White Witch was bad and cruel. (pp. 85-86)

Edmund's efforts to excuse his action show that he is aware of a standard of conduct he is violating, and that he, like the readers who judge him, uses that standard as the basis of acceptable behavior.

Thus, long before the term "Deep Magic" is used, the concept it images—the rules of fair play and straight dealing—has been introduced. For Deep Magic is what in our world is called the Law of Nature, or as Lewis phrases it in *Mere Christianity,* "the Law of *Human* Nature," the law or rule about right and wrong which "every one [knows] by nature and [does] not need to be taught" (p. 18). Through "Deep Magic" Lewis is depicting in a form which appeals to imagination and emotion, in a form children can relate to, what he had described conceptually in the opening chapters of *Mere Christianity:*

> Now what interests me about [such remarks as "How'd you like it if anyone did the same to you?" and "Come on, you promised"] is that the man who makes them is not merely saying that the other man's behaviour does not happen to please him. He is appealing to some kind of standard of behaviour which he expects the other man to know about. . . . It looks, in fact, very much as if both parties had in mind some kind of Law or Rule of fair play or decent behaviour or morality or whatever you like to call it, about which they really agreed. And they have. (p. 17)

Deep Magic, like the Law of Nature, is universal: it applies to Narnians and humans alike and is associated with two major earthly mythologies. It is written on a Stone Table, recalling the Old Testament tablets of stone with their superb statement of natural law, and it is carved "in letters deep as a spear is long on the trunk of the World Ash Tree" (p. 138), a symbol of the origin and foundation of the world in the Icelandic myths. It is of divine origin—the "Emperor's magic" (p. 140), "engraved on the sceptre of the Emperor-Beyond-the-Sea" (p. 138)—but it is not co-existent with the Emperor: it has existed only from the Dawn of Time. It was created with the universe, as a magic which makes moral and social order in the universe possible. Aslan himself ranks adherence to and preservation of it very high: " 'Work against the Emperor's magic?' said Aslan turning to [Susan] with something like a frown on his face. And nobody ever made that suggestion to him again" (p. 140). And in Narnia as on Earth, undermining the Magic, now referred to as "the Law," will lead to chaos: "Unless I have blood as the Law says," the Witch declares, "all Narnia will be overturned and perish in fire and water" (p. 139).

The concept of the Law of Nature was very important to Lewis, as it was to Plato, Aristotle, Aquinas, and Hooker before him. It appears repeatedly elsewhere in his fiction. In *Out of the Silent Planet* Lewis asserts that it is not limited to our world but is true for rational creatures on other planets as well. The Oyarsa of Malacandra says to Ransom, "There are laws that all *hnau* know, of pity and straight dealing and shame and the like."[4] In *That Hideous Strength* those laws are embodied in the attitude that pervades the Manor at St. Anne's, as Ransom and his followers seek to adhere to the outlook of his "Masters." Ransom says of them, "They are not old fashioned: but they are very very old."[5] These old, but not old-fashioned, precepts Lewis calls, in his most important nonfiction work, the Tao, "the doctrine of objective value, the belief that certain attitudes are really true, and others really false, to the kind of thing the universe is and the kind of things we are."[6] Elsewhere he elaborates on the implications of that definition: "We have only two alternatives. Either the maxims of traditional morality must be accepted as axioms of practical reason which neither admit nor require argument to support them and not to 'see' which is to have lost human status; or else there are no values at all."[7] So important is belief in such objective values in Lewis's way of thinking that he calls belief in subjective values (a growing tendency in our times) "the disease that will certainly end our species (and, in my view, damn our souls) if it is not crushed."[8]

The law alone is stern and unrelenting. In *Mere Christianity* Lewis writes, "There is nothing indulgent about the Moral Law. It is as hard as nails. It tells you to do the straight thing and it does not seem to care how painful, or dangerous, or difficult it is to do" (p. 37). The Stone Table, when the children first see it in *The Lion, the Witch and the Wardrobe,* is "a great grim slab of grey stone" (p. 121). Thus, after Edmund is rescued from the clutches of the White Witch by Aslan's forces, the Witch can claim, justly (no one can put more emphasis on the justness of a thing than a tyrant, if the thing fits his or her purposes), that Edmund must die: "Every traitor belongs to me as my lawful prey and . . . for every treachery I have a right to a kill" (p. 139). Lewis chose the most fundamental and universal element of the moral code, the forbidding of treachery, as his key: all societies condemn treason and through most of history have assigned the death penalty to it. To Lewis's readers, children as well as adults, the justice of it all is apparent. Edmund's life is, justly, forfeit. Deep Magic, the Law of Nature upon which an orderly and just society rests, demands it.

In the magical world of Narnia, then, one discovers the importance of Deep Magic, of the same natural laws as in our world—known, but not kept, by all. Transcending Deep Magic, however, is another magic, a Deeper Magic from before the dawn of time, a magic inherent not in created things but in their creator, the greater magic of grace. That Deep Magic appears in the story before Deeper Magic is important. They must be considered in that order, Lewis had said in his radio talks, for the latter to make sense: "It is after you have realised that there is a real Moral Law, and a Power behind the law, and that you have broken that law and put yourself wrong with that Power—it is after all this, and not a moment sooner, that Christianity begins to talk" *(Mere Christianity,* pp. 38-39). So it is too in Narnia. Readers of *The Lion, the Witch and the Wardrobe* are first made aware of the fundamental moral law—made aware by recognizing Edmund's unfairness first to Lucy and then to the others—*in order that* Aslan's death may convey its full meaning.

Aslan, out of his love or grace—the Deeper Magic—agrees to meet the Witch's demands by dying in Edmund's place. He slips away from the good Narnians' tent at night, but is followed by Lucy and Susan, from whose viewpoint the episode is related. They see Aslan walk up to and allow himself to be taken by such people as "Ogres with monstrous teeth, and wolves, and bull-headed men . . . [and] Cruels and Hags and Incubuses, Wraiths, Horrors, Efreets, Sprites, Orknies, Wooses, and Ettins."

> They rolled the huge Lion round on his back and tied all his four paws together, shouting and cheering as if they had done something brave, though, had the Lion chosen, one of those paws could have been the death of them all. But he made no noise, even when the enemies, straining and tugging, pulled the cords so tight that they cut into his flesh. Then they began to drag him towards the Stone Table.
>
> "Stop!" said the Witch. "Let him first be shaved."
>
> Another roar of mean laughter went up from her followers as an ogre with a pair of shears came forward and squatted down by Aslan's head. Snip-snip-snip went the shears and masses of curling gold began to fall to the ground. Then the ogre stood back and the children, watching from their hiding-place, could see the face of Aslan looking all small and different without its mane. The enemies also saw the difference.
>
> "Why, he's only a great cat after all!" cried one.
>
> "Is *that* what we were afraid of?" said another.
>
> And they surged round Aslan jeering at him, saying things

like "Puss, Puss! Poor Pussy," and "How many mice have you caught to-day, Cat?" and "Would you like a saucer of milk, Pussums?"

"Oh how *can* they?" said Lucy, tears streaming down her cheeks. "The brutes, the brutes!" for now that the first shock was over the shorn face of Aslan looked to her braver, and more beautiful, and more patient than ever.

"Muzzle him!" said the Witch. And even now, as they worked about his face putting on the muzzle, one bite from his jaws would have cost two or three of them their hands. But he never moved. And this seemed to enrage all that rabble. Everyone was at him now. Those who had been afraid to come near him even after he was bound began to find their courage, and for a few minutes the two girls could not even see him—so thickly was he surrounded by the whole crowd of creatures kicking him, hitting him, spitting on him, jeering at him. (pp. 148-51)

This is the most nearly allegorical episode in the Chronicles. The willing sacrifice, the biblical tone and imagery (it reminds me especially of Isaiah 53: "He was oppressed and afflicted, yet he opened not his mouth"), and Aslan's subsequent return to life clearly associate him with Christ. Yet, Lewis insisted that it was not allegorical but suppositional: suppose there was a world like Narnia and that Christ chose to be incarnate and die and rise again in that world, this is what it might have been like. Given this approach, the meaning of Aslan's death should be comprehensible in terms of the secondary world Lewis created and not be dependent on reference to another, or primary, world for clarity or effect. The general meaning of Aslan's death is very similar to the meaning of the death of Christ in our world, but one does not need to know or refer to the story of Christ to gain that meaning. The story itself, by its structural movement from Deep Magic to Deeper Magic, conveys the magic of grace, which is more important here than the idea or theology behind that magic. Aslan does not "stand for" Christ; in his suppositional world he *is* Christ. His death in Narnia is similar to his death in our world because both are examples of the same archetype, of the dying and returning god. And the myth in which his story is recounted conveys the basic meanings of that archetype, the divine truths of love, sacrifice, and hope.

Aslan's death has two divinely magical effects. First, it puts the Law in a new perspective. At Aslan's resurrection, "the Stone Table was broken into two pieces by a great crack that ran down it from end to end" (p. 158). Previously the Witch could claim the "proper use" of the Stone Table was the execution of traitors; a broken table cannot be effective for, or symbolic of, that old use. Second, it changes the meaning and effect of death. As Aslan romps with Susan and Lucy after his return to life, he explains that, if the White Witch had known about Deeper Magic, "she would have known that when a willing victim who had committed no treachery was killed in a traitor's stead, the Table would crack and Death itself would start working backwards" (p. 160). The effect of Deeper Magic, then, is to give life. The direct recipient of this life is, of course, Edmund, whose life is saved by Aslan's sacrifice. Before Aslan goes to his death, he walks apart with Edmund for a "conversation which Edmund never forgot" (p. 135). It apparently was not about the arrangement Aslan was soon to make with the Witch; Edmund may in fact never have been told about that (p. 177). The important thing is that Edmund comes to know Aslan, and to love him. As a result of that and of his experiences in Narnia, Edmund gets past "thinking about himself" and just goes on "looking at Aslan" (p. 138). Edmund's life is spared physically and healed spiritually: Lucy finds him "not only healed of his wounds but looking better than she had seen him look—oh, for ages. . . . He had become his real old self again and could look you in the face" (p. 177). Edmund's experiences continue to have a significant influence upon his character thereafter, one that is reflected in the name he is given later as one of the monarchs of Narnia: "Edmund was a graver and quieter man than Peter, and great in council and judgement. He was called King Edmund the Just" (p. 181). He who has had a personal experience with justice—and its counterpart of grace—is best able to appreciate its proper use and value.

The magic of story and narrative, of Deep and Deeper Magic, are, finally, unified by the vehicle Lewis used for the story, the traditional mode of the romance. *The Lion, the Witch and the Wardrobe,* like most romances, presents a series of adventures with a goal, overthrowing the White Witch; the goal is apparently frustrated by the death of the hero in the showdown scene, but it is ultimately achieved after the hero's return. The plot pattern, character types, and details in the story (swords, battles, magic) are all characteristic of romance. The romantic mode is emphasized—even exaggerated—in the final chapter of the book, as the children appear "in their hunting array" (p. 185), with a "different style" of talking ("Fair Consorts, let us now alight from our horses and follow this beast into the thicket"—p. 182). The importance of the mode appears in two ways. Northrop Frye calls romance "the story of summer," the mode which pictures idealized human experience and its wish-fulfillment dream of complete happiness; its antithetical counterpart, antiromance, "the story of winter," portrays unideal experience and is an anxiety dream of total bondage and frustration. Lewis's use of winter and spring, then, which works so well to convey to children imaginatively and emotionally a world dominated by evil and a world luxuriating in good, takes on a deeper significance as part of an ages-old pattern of basic human response to nature and life. Inherent in the romance form, furthermore, is the assumption of an order in and above the world, a sense of unity and of immanent meaning in the universe. The theme of justice, needed simply to set up the events of the story, also assumes and points toward the kind of transcendent order on which the romance form has been based for thousands of years. Providing, imaginatively, a sense of that order and an acquaintance with the persons behind it—Aslan and the Emperor—is a large part of the ultimate purpose of the story. The form and theme of *The Lion, the Witch and the Wardrobe* unite, as if by magic, in the romance archetype and its antithesis, in the movement from unideal to ideal, from perpetual winter to lasting spring, from the disorder and bondage of the Witch's rule to the ultimate order, freedom, and fulfillment of Aslan's rule.

The meaning and method of the first Chronicle of Narnia are epitomized shortly after Aslan's resurrection when he and the two girls rush to the Witch's castle and Aslan begins to breathe on the "courtyard full of statues" they find there (p. 163). "Everywhere the statues were coming to life. The courtyard looked no longer like a museum; it looked more like a zoo" (p. 166). Those who were trapped in stone by the demands of the Stone Table are given new life by the effects of the Deeper Magic. Lewis echoes here his own analogy in *Mere Christianity,* where he says that receiving *Zoe,* the spiritual life which is in God from all eternity, would be comparable to a statue being changed from carved stone to a real man: "And that is precisely what Christianity is about. This world is a great sculptor's shop. We are the statues and there is a rumour going round the shop that some of us are some day going to come to life" (p. 140). What was metaphor in *Mere Christianity* becomes reality in Narnia—the idea is transformed into image. And that is what happens in *The Lion, the Witch and the Wardrobe* as a whole. In relating the myth about Aslan, Lewis presents the basic ideas of the Christian faith in our world, transformed into the images and actions of another world. The movement of the plot parallels closely the progression of the ideas in *The Case for Christianity* (the first two sections of *Mere Christianity):* that there are ideas of right behavior known to all; that people do not practice the sort of behavior they know is right; that such disobedience puts them wrong with the law and the power behind the law, without the ability to put themselves right; and that Christ's death has somehow put them right again and given them a fresh start. The structure of the story captures, for the imagination, the shape of the Christian message and presents it as true in Narnia as well: law first, then release, through sacrifice and love; first Deep Magic, then Deeper Magic. Through the enchanting power of the fairy tale, through the elvish magic of image and myth, *The Lion, the Witch and the Wardrobe* conveys a message about divine magic in a form that children can grasp and identify with more easily than the biblical account, and in a way that revitalizes for older readers as well truths and feelings which have become obscured by familiarity and repetition.

3

"Finding Out by Experience": Belief and Disbelief in *Prince Caspian*

*T*HE second of the Chronicles of Narnia, *Prince Caspian,* is an initiation tale, the story of a young person leaving a sheltered, often ideal environment to encounter the harsh realities of the world and through them to grow to maturity. It is a basic romance motif, often repeated in literature, because it is a universal element of human experience. Thus the tale follows Caspian from his childhood, spent listening to stories told by his nurse at the castle, where he slept between silken sheets and ate from gold and silver dishes (p. 79), through his series of adventures in the woods and as a leader in battle, to the moment when the High King Peter, at Aslan's command, "bestowed Knighthood of the Order of the Lion" on him (p. 204). Caspian has taken at least the first steps toward maturity when Aslan greets and questions him near the end of the book:

> "Welcome, Prince," said Aslan. "Do you feel yourself sufficient to take up the Kingship of Narnia?"
> "I—I don't think I do, Sir," said Caspian. "I'm only a kid."
> "Good," said Aslan. "If you had felt yourself sufficient, it would have been proof that you were not. Therefore, under us and under the High King, you shall be King of Narnia, Lord

of Cair Paravel and Emperor of the Lone Islands. You and
your heirs while your race lasts." (p. 200)

Prince Caspian, thus, provides the frame which gives the
story a beginning, middle, and end. The unity of this story,
however, is not found in its plot, but in its "heroic" tone;
as the tone fuses with the sequence of events in the plot,
it develops also the underlying theme of trust in Aslan.

The tone of heroism is present from the beginning, with
its emphasis on ancient times, the heroic age of Narnia.
Although the first three chapters occur in the present and
describe the arrival of the Pevensies in Narnia, the discovery of the ruins of Cair Paravel, and the rescue of
Trumpkin the dwarf, their concern is primarily with the
past. Their setting is the ruins of an old castle, which reminds the children of former days: "How it all comes back,"
Lucy exclaims (p. 13). The discovery of the golden chess
piece the children had used centuries before ("It brought
back—oh, such lovely times"—p. 16), of the apple orchard
they helped plant in the past ("Don't you remember?"—
p. 18), and of the ancient treasure chamber containing the
gifts Aslan gave them long ago ("There was something sad
and a little frightening about the place, because it all
seemed so forsaken and long ago"—p. 22) capture the feeling of "pastness," of antiquity. It is summed up as Susan
twangs her bowstring "and that one small noise brought
back the old days to the children's minds more than anything that had happened yet" (p. 25). The details and rem-
iniscences have taken the children and the readers back
to the heroic age of Narnia, the age of armor and knights
and treasures, of "battles and hunts and feasts" (p. 25).

The "old days" also dominate the chapters which introduce the hero of the story. Trumpkin the dwarf, in a four-
chapter flashback, recounts Caspian's childhood at the new
castle, his escape when a son is born to the usurper Miraz,
his reception by the Old Narnians in the forest, his early,

unsuccessful, efforts in the war against Miraz's forces, and his decision to blow Susan's horn in hopes of receiving help from Aslan. Again the sense of a past, and nostalgia for it, dominate the tone: "I wish—I wish—I wish I could have lived in the Old Days," Caspian remarks to his uncle (p. 38), and Doctor Cornelius urges Caspian to try to be "a King like the High King Peter of old" in "the Golden Age in Narnia" (p. 50). The past is emphasized as the Old Narnians establish their headquarters in a mound "raised in very ancient times" (p. 85), one which seems "to belong to an even older Narnia" (p. 86) than what Caspian had been told about before, and as they decide to blow the magic horn of Queen Susan, "which she left behind her when she vanished from Narnia at the end of the Golden Age" (p. 58). While the opening seven chapters are important, then, for filling in the background of Caspian's story, they are equally important in creating "a great longing for the old days when the trees could talk in Narnia" (p. 112).

At first glance the first half of the book, with its four-chapter flashback, seems rather cumbersome. But that structure has a purpose, beyond allowing the action to begin "in the middle of things." The opening three chapters provide readers a touchstone by which to judge the stories of the past referred to in the following four chapters. The relics of the past which the children discover, as well as their very presence in Narnia, attest to the truth of the old stories, unlikely as they seem. Although some characters always believed the old stories ("Best of badgers," says Peter to Trufflehunter, "you never doubted us all through"— p. 168), most experience doubt to a greater or lesser extent; but the reader knows, because of the details in the opening three chapters, how groundless all those doubts, and perhaps all such doubts, really are. Upon that foundation a debate between belief and disbelief is based, a debate which develops into a key theme of the book. The word "believe" is used for the first time as Peter delivers his fourth point to prove that the ruins they discovered are those of Cair Paravel: "Can you have forgotten that funny old Lily-gloves, the chief mole, leaning on his spade and saying, 'Believe me, your Majesty, you'll be glad of these fruit trees one day.' And by Jove he was right" (p. 18). It is repeated often, especially in developing three main examples of disbelief.

The first is Caspian's uncle, the usurper, King Miraz. When Caspian tells his uncle the stories he has heard, of a witch and a long winter, of two boys and two girls who became kings and queens, and of a great lion called Aslan, Miraz labels the stories "fairy tales" (p. 39) and declares, "There never were those Kings and Queens. . . . And there's no such person as Aslan. And there are no such things as lions. And there never was a time when animals could talk. Do you hear?" (p. 40). Caspian is informed later, by his tutor, Doctor Cornelius, that all this is a rejection by Miraz of what he knows to be true, rather than an inability to believe: "It is you Telmarines who silenced the beasts and the trees and the fountains, and who killed and drove away the dwarfs and fauns, and are now trying to cover up even the memory of them. The King does not allow them to be spoken of" (p. 47). As a part of this rejection of truth, this obscuring and hiding of reality, the Telmarines have made up stories about ghosts haunting the woods and waters: "Your Kings are in deadly fear of the sea because they can never quite forget that in all stories Aslan comes from over the sea. They don't want to go near it and they don't want anyone else to go near it. So they have let great woods grow up to cut their people off from the coast. But because they have quarrelled with the trees they are afraid of the woods. And because they are afraid of the woods they imagine that they are full of ghosts. And the Kings and great men, hating both the sea and the wood, partly believe these stories, and partly encourage them" (pp. 50-51). In their efforts to avoid believing the truth the

Telmarines created falsehoods and, ironically, have begun
to believe them. In the end, Miraz is caught by his efforts
to obscure reality. After Edmund has delivered the challenge from Peter, Miraz responds to his advisors Glozelle
and Sopespian:

> "King Edmund, pah!" said Miraz. "Does your Lordship be-
> lieve those old wives' fables about Peter and Edmund and the
> rest?"
> "I believe my eyes, your Majesty," said Glozelle. (p. 177)

Having blotted out the past, having refused to learn from
the old stories about Aslan's power, Miraz lets himself be
tricked into accepting the challenge which leads directly
to his death.

The second example of disbelief is Trumpkin, the Red
Dwarf, who, with Nikabrik the Black Dwarf and Trufflehunter the Badger, finds Caspian, injured while fleeing
from Miraz, and nurses him back to health. As Caspian
relates his story and the others discuss it, the name of the
High King Peter is mentioned.

> "Do you believe all those old stories?" asked Trumpkin.
> "I tell you, we don't change, we beasts," said Trufflehunter.
> "We don't forget. I believe in the High King Peter and the
> rest that reigned at Cair Paravel, as firmly as I believe in
> Aslan himself."
> "As firmly as *that,* I daresay," said Trumpkin. "But who
> believes in Aslan nowadays?"
> "I do," said Caspian. "And if I hadn't believed in him be-
> fore, I would now. Back there among the Humans the people
> who laughed at Aslan would have laughed at stories about
> talking beasts and Dwarfs. Sometimes I did wonder if there
> really was such a person as Aslan: but then sometimes I won-
> dered if there were really people like you. Yet there you are."
> (p. 66)

Lewis reflects here his usual premise, that most things
people believe are based on faith rather than demonstra-
tion. Caspian and Trufflehunter are willing to accept that

and get on with living. But Trumpkin will not believe without being shown. He does not believe in walking trees (pp. 76-77), or in the horn (pp. 90, 92) even when the children have appeared:

> "Great Scott," said Peter. "So it was the horn—your own horn, Su—that dragged us all off that seat on the platform yesterday morning! I can hardly believe it; yet it all fits in."
>
> "I don't know why you shouldn't believe it," said Lucy, "if you believe in magic at all." (p. 96)

But Trumpkin does not believe in magic, or in the children. Only when he is shown—by being disarmed by Edmund in a fencing match, outdone by Susan in an archery contest, and cured by a drop of cordial from Lucy's diamond bottle—will he accept the children as the true kings and queens of old:

> "And now," said Peter, "if you've really decided to believe in us—"
>
> "I have," said the Dwarf. (p. 104)

But he is not willing to generalize from that experience. Although he will accept the children and travel with them to join Caspian, his other doubts continue, until he can be shown by a more startling experience.

The third example of disbelief is Nikabrik, who, Caspian remarks later, "had gone sour inside from long suffering and hating" (p. 168). When Caspian asks if he believes in Aslan, he replies, "I'll believe in anyone or anything . . . that'll batter these cursed Telmarine barbarians to pieces or drive them out of Narnia. Anyone or anything. Aslan *or* the White Witch, do you understand?" (p. 73). Although Trumpkin, as we have seen, is a skeptic, his values are sound; he retains a clear perspective on things and lives by the moral law. That is not the case with Nikabrik, who, unlike Trumpkin and the others, is quite willing to have "an Ogre or two and a Hag" on their side in the battle

(p. 72). The contrast between the two dwarfs is shown by
their reactions to the moonlight dance on Dancing Lawn.
Dance has been, traditionally, a symbol of harmony and
order, in the universe, society, and individuals. It is significant, then, that Trumpkin joins in, awkwardly to be
sure, but Nikabrik will have nothing to do with it all:
"Before [Caspian] knew what he was doing he found himself joining in the dance. Trumpkin, with heavier and jerk-
ier movements, did likewise and even Trufflehunter
hopped and lumbered about as best he could. Only Nikabrik stayed where he was, looking on in silence" (p. 78).
Trumpkin doubts, but Nikabrik despairs, and out of his
despair he brings a hag and a werewolf to the leaders'
council and prepares to commit treason against his King
by having them call up the White Witch of old: "Don't all
take fright at a name as if you were children. We want
power: and we want a power that will be on our side. . . .
They say she ruled for a hundred years: a hundred years
of winter. There's power, if you like. There's something
practical" (pp. 162-63). In the ensuing skirmish, Nikabrik
is killed, and Caspian expresses regrets: "If we had won
quickly he might have become a good Dwarf in the days
of peace" (p. 168). Perhaps so. But there was in him an
attitude that led others to grief as well: only two other
characters are associated with practicality—Miraz is shown
to be practical on pages 55-56 and Susan is said to be practical on page 117. This is not to say, surely, that belief
necessarily implies impracticality; but it does suggest that
belief cannot be entirely safe or self-interested. Trumpkin
finally becomes willing to risk himself, his total identity,
in a way that Miraz, Nikabrik, and Susan (eventually)
were not willing to.

An initiation story often includes the hero's movement
toward spiritual as well as physical and emotional maturity. In *Prince Caspian,* however, the spiritual development is experienced not by the hero but by those who are

searching for the hero. After Trumpkin has decided to believe in the children, Peter declares, "It's quite clear what
we have to do. We must join King Caspian at once" (p. 104).
For the children and the dwarf, the journey they undertake
to join Caspian is also a spiritual journey, a journey into
faith.

They leave the island by boat, choosing their own
course—along the coast and up Glasswater Creek—and
relying upon their own efforts. Although the first leg of the
journey goes well, they are left feeling discouraged and
uncertain: "Up till now the children had only been thinking of how to get to Caspian. Now they wondered what
they would do when they found him, and how a handful of
Dwarfs and woodland creatures could defeat an army of
grown-up humans" (pp. 109-10). In their own strength, of
course, they could not; yet they do not seek help beyond
their own resources: "You've got that pocket-compass of
yours, Peter, haven't you? Well then, we're as right as rain.
We've only got to keep on going North-West—cross that
little river, the what-do-you-call-it? . . . Cross it and strike
up hill, and we'll be at the Stone Table (Aslan's How, I
mean) by eight or nine o'clock" (p. 114). Edmund's slip in
referring to their destination by its old name, the Stone
Table, instead of by its new name, Aslan's How, anticipates
a problem, however. Things have changed since the heroic
age of the children's previous visit to Narnia, and Peter
eventually has to admit, "We're lost. I've never seen this
place in my life before" (p. 119). At that point Lucy, the
youngest of the children and the one least involved in making the decisions, sees Aslan, indicating, by his expression,
that he wants them to go the opposite direction from the
one they have chosen. The others prefer, however, to rely
on their own judgments and go their own way: the result
is a long, tiring walk, an attack by some sentries of Miraz,
and a time-wasting return along the way they had come.

That night Aslan awakens Lucy from a deep sleep and

teaches her a valuable lesson about commitment. She begins defending herself for going along with the others and ends up realizing that often, in crucial matters, one must go it alone: "I couldn't have left the others and come up to you alone, how could I? Don't look at me like that . . . oh well, I suppose I *could*. Yes, and it wouldn't have been alone, I know, not if I was with you" (p. 137). She then is told to act upon that lesson: "Go back to the others now, and wake them up; and tell them you have seen me again; and that you must all get up at once and follow me—what will happen? There is only one way of finding out" (p. 137). The word "wake" invites a figurative reading as well as the literal one and, together with the allusion to Christ's words directing his disciples to "follow me," it confirms the spiritual aspect of the journey. The episode conveys the essence of trust, especially in the instructions Aslan gives to Lucy: if the others will not come, Aslan says, "then you at least must follow me alone" (p. 139). Actions in Narnia once again reflect the ideas of *Mere Christianity*. Lewis wrote there that at some point in the process of moving toward Christian maturity, we must undergo either suddenly or gradually a change "from being confident about our own efforts to the state in which we despair of doing anything for ourselves and leave it to God" (p. 128). We cannot, Lewis asserts, get into the right relation with God until we have discovered that fact of our bankruptcy: "When I say 'discovered,' I mean really discovered: . . . really finding out by experience that it is true" (p. 127). The children and Trumpkin make that discovery. They have tried their hardest and have failed; now they must admit their defeat, accept their inadequacies, and hand themselves over to Aslan.

As Lucy tries to get the other children and the dwarf to accompany her, Lewis uses, as he does elsewhere in depicting faith, a play on the phrase "seeing is believing." In Lewis's version, those who believe are able to see; those who do not believe cannot see—that, he writes in a note commenting on *Till We Have Faces,* is "the way the thing must have been."[1] When Aslan instructs Lucy to go to the others and tell them to follow him, she asks, "Will the others see you too?" His reply is, "Certainly not at first. . . . Later on, it depends" (pp. 137-38). The image is the same Lewis would use later in *The Last Battle* and again in *Till We Have Faces.* In the former, the dwarfs do not see Aslan or the feast he offers them because they do not believe in him or his gifts. In the latter, Orual is unable to see the palace in which Psyche lives with her divine spouse because Orual is unable to believe in the gods or in the palace. What a person sees depends on who he or she is and what he or she is looking for, as Uncle Andrew demonstrates in *The Magician's Nephew* (p. 125). Because Lucy's companions do not believe Aslan is present, they do not see him. They are greatly confused ("Why should Aslan be invisible to us? He never used to be"—p. 142) and even angry ("There isn't anything to see. She's been dreaming"— p. 141) at their inability to see Aslan, but at last they do come, a first step of faith. Initially, of course, they are just following Lucy: "The others had only Lucy's directions to guide them, for Aslan was not only invisible to them but silent as well" (pp. 143-44). As they do follow her and as they are led successfully down a steep cliff and across a roaring river, their trust increases and first Edmund and Peter, then Susan, and finally even Trumpkin are able to see him.

Susan and Trumpkin provide an interesting contrast as they come to accept Aslan. Susan believed all along in Aslan's existence, but her emotions kept her from putting her trust in him: "I've been far worse than you know. I really believed it was him—he, I mean—yesterday. When he warned us not to go down to the fir-wood. And I really believed it was him tonight, when you woke us up. I mean, deep down inside. Or I could have, if I'd let myself. But I just wanted to get out of the woods and—and—oh, I don't know. And what ever am I to say to him?" (p. 147). It is the sort of situation Lewis warned the Christian in our world about when he wrote, in *Mere Christianity,* "The battle is between faith and reason on one side and emotion and imagination on the other" (p. 122). Aslan recognizes and ministers to her problem in just that light: " 'You have listened to fears, child,' said Aslan. 'Come, let me breathe on you' " (p. 148). Trumpkin, on the other hand, continues to the end to assert his disbelief: "I have no use for magic lions which are talking lions and don't talk, and friendly lions though they don't do us any good, and whopping big lions though nobody can see them. It's all bilge and bean-stalks as far as I can see" (p. 142). Trumpkin, doubting Thomas that he is, again must be shown before he will believe, and Aslan ministers to him in his weakness ac-cordingly: "And now, where is this little Dwarf, this fa-mous swordsman and archer, who doesn't believe in lions?" (p. 148). By taking Trumpkin and tossing him high into the air, as one might do with a child, Aslan makes the dwarf physically dependent upon him: "The Dwarf flew up in the air. He was as safe as if he had been in bed, though he did not feel so. As he came down the huge velveted paws caught him as gently as a mother's arms and set him (right way up, too) on the ground" (p. 149). Having seen Aslan, Trumpkin believes; having, without choice, been forced to "leave it" to Aslan, he is ready to move on and act upon his faith.

In describing Christian belief early in *Mere Christian-ity,* Lewis uses this metaphor: "Enemy-occupied territory— that is what this world is. Christianity is the story of how the rightful king has landed, you might say landed in disguise, and is calling us all to take part in a great campaign of sabotage" (p. 51). In a sense this is the image behind the plot of *Prince Caspian* as a whole, as the right-ful kings and queens, including Aslan, "the highest of all

High Kings" *(The Voyage of the "Dawn Treader,"* p. 135),
land in Narnia and conduct a campaign against enemy
forces who occupy the land. The effect of that image comes
through particularly after the children and the lion arrive
at Aslan's How. The campaign of sabotage takes two strik-
ingly different directions. The first is battle. Peter and Edmund, after putting down the insurrection by Nikabrik,
arrange—with the help of some duplicity within the enemy ranks—a single combat between Peter and Miraz. The
challenge reminds the reader again of the past, as Peter
"recalled to his mind the language in which he had written
such things long ago in Narnia's golden age" (pp. 171-72).
The scene—from the wording of the challenge, to the as-
signment of marshals, to the fight itself, to Peter's courtesy
as "a Knight" (p. 189)—is straight out of the romance tradition. The combat ends, however, very unheroically—
through villainy on the part of the Telmarines: " 'To arms,
Narnia. Treachery!' Peter shouted" (p. 189). In a story whose
theme has been belief and faith, in a genre based on a code
which emphasized honor above all else, the deciding inci-
dents, ironically, proceed through a series of violations of
trust: the insubordination and rebellion of Nikabrik, the
treachery of Glozelle and Sopespian in goading Miraz into
fighting and in attacking the Narnians before the combat
has ended, and the infidelity of Glozelle in stabbing the
fallen Miraz in the back. The Telmarines' lack of belief in
Aslan is reflected in their lack of respect for their fellow
creatures, as it has been, in fact, ever since they entered
Narnia.

The second direction in which the campaign of sabotage
moves is revelry. Dance has appeared throughout the story
as a symbol of harmony (pp. 45-46) and of a proper response to Aslan—the dance of the fauns in Chapter 6 and
the dance of the trees in Chapter 10 anticipate the wild
romp which begins in Chapter 11 and continues in Chapter
14. Imagery of dance is common in Lewis's fiction, but it

is complicated here by the introduction of "a youth, dressed only in a fawn-skin, with vine-leaves wreathed in his curly hair" (p. 152). He is Bacchus, the Greek god of wine and revelry, who, with his strange company of maenads, satyrs, and sileni, had been a frequent visitor in Narnia in its heroic age: "[In] summer when the woods were green . . . old Silenus on his fat donkey would come to visit them, and sometimes Bacchus himself, and then the streams would run with wine instead of water and the whole forest would give itself up to jollification for weeks on end" *(The Lion, the Witch, and the Wardrobe,* p. 13). Lewis introduces him here to reinforce and expand the sense of joy and freedom as the invaders liberate the occupied territories. The use of Bacchus presents its dangers; the Greeks recognized the harmful potential of wine and Bacchus was characterized by drunken frenzy and cruelty as well as by release and mirthmaking. The story acknowledges those dangers in Susan's remark,

> "I wouldn't have felt very safe with Bacchus and all his wild girls if we'd met them without Aslan."
> "I should think not," said Lucy. (p. 154)

With Bacchus under the restraints of Aslan's greater power, however, he can be used to symbolize the meaning of Aslan's coming. Part of what Bacchus adds comes through in Edith Hamilton's description of the Bacchic festivals in later Greek history: "No other festival in Greece could compare with it. It took place in the spring when the vine begins to put forth its branches, and it lasted for five days. They were days of perfect peace and enjoyment. All the ordinary business of life stopped. No one could be put in prison; prisoners were even released so that they could share in the general rejoicing."[2] Lewis draws on the joy, change, and freedom traditionally associated with Bacchus to celebrate the restoration of "the long-lost days of freedom" in Narnia (p. 48).

The celebration begins with a wild romp: "But nearly everyone seemed to have a different idea as to what they were playing. It may have been Tig, but Lucy never discovered who was It. It was rather like Blind Man's Buff, only everyone behaved as if he was blindfolded. It was not unlike Hunt the Slipper, but the slipper was never found" (p. 152). Later Aslan declares a holiday and the whole party moves off, "Aslan leading, Bacchus and his Maenads leaping, rushing, and turning somersaults, the beasts frisking round them, and Silenus and his donkey bringing up the rear" (p. 192). The freedom within that company soon reaches out to others—first to the Beruna River:

> Before they had begun to cross [the bridge], however, up out of the water came a great wet, bearded head, larger than a man's, crowned with rushes. It looked at Aslan and out of its mouth a deep voice came.
>
> "Hail, Lord," it said. "Loose my chains."
>
> "Who on earth is *that?*" whispered Susan.
>
> "I think it's the river-god, but hush," said Lucy.
>
> "Bacchus," said Aslan. "Deliver him from his chains."
>
> "That means the bridge, I expect," thought Lucy. And so it did. (pp. 192-93)

Soon strong trunks of ivy and other vegetation cover the bridge, break it down, and give the river its freedom. "Wherever they went in the little town of Beruna it was the same" (p. 195). The coming of Aslan liberates ("Chained dogs broke their chains"—p. 195), comforts ("The boy, who had been crying a moment before, burst out laughing and joined them"—p. 195), and heals ("Why I do declare I feel *that* better. I think I could take a little breakfast this morning"—p. 197).

The battle and revelry, then, are contrasting but complementary actions, together defeating the Telmarine forces which had "silenced the beasts and the trees and the fountains, and ... killed and [driven] away the dwarfs and fauns" (p. 47) and which had enslaved the spirits of their own people by wiping out the very memory of Aslan and all that he stood for. Contrasting responses to Aslan's offer of freedom are illustrated by the two schoolteachers whom the revelers encounter. "The first house they came to was a school: a girl's school, where a lot of Narnian girls, with their hair done very tight and ugly tight collars round their necks and thick tickly stockings on their legs, were having a history lesson" (pp. 193-94). The confinement and repression are symbolized by the girls' clothes and by the history lesson, for Caspian's education much earlier illustrated the New Narnian use of history. Miss Prizzle, the teacher, after reprimanding Gwendolen for looking out the window and talking nonsense about a lion, sees her tidy schoolhouse dissolve into a forest glade and flees from nature and freedom with her class—except for Gwendolen, who joins the dance and is released from some of the "unnecessary and uncomfortable" clothes she was wearing (p. 195). In contrast to Miss Prizzle's response is that at another school, "where a tired-looking girl was teaching arithmetic to a number of boys who looked very like pigs. She looked out of the window and saw the divine revellers . . . and a stab of joy went through her heart" (p. 196). After Bacchus frightens off her insolent, belligerent pupils and turns them externally into the pigs they already were internally, she yields to the divine longing within her, jumps down, and joins the celebration. "And so at last, with leaping and dancing and singing, with music and laughter and roaring and barking and neighing, they all came to the place where Miraz's army stood flinging down their swords and holding up their hands" (p. 198) and the two parts of the campaign of sabotage are united in victory.

In the final chapter, the celebration of the victory of Old Narnia over the New concludes with a dance and a feast, and the earlier themes are reiterated. The hero is given renewed attention when his history as a member of the Telmarine race is recounted (pp. 210-12); the theme of faith is reasserted by the reaction of the Telmarines to the door Aslan set up for passage back to an island in the Pacific: "We don't see any other world through those sticks. If you want us to believe in it, why doesn't one of *you* go?" (p. 213); and the heroic tone is reemphasized by Reepicheep's quick response, "If *my* example can be of any service, Aslan, . . . I will take eleven mice through that arch at your bidding without a moment's delay" (p. 213). The ending unifies the plot and themes of the book, but does not complete the story of the growth of the hero—the cycle of Caspian's life extends into the next two books. *Prince Caspian* describes Caspian's initiation and the first steps toward his maturity: he rides off from his sheltered, secure homelife "to seek adventures" (p. 59) and as a result he is said later to be hardened "and his face wore a kinglier look" (p. 79). But that kingliness does not come through strongly in this story: Caspian's leadership of the army is on the whole unsuccessful; Peter takes command after his arrival at Aslan's How; and Peter, not Caspian, fights the decisive, character-testing duel. Rather than stressing the heroism of the prince, Lewis subordinates his title character in the second half of the book in order to emphasize the theme of faith. As a result, the theme of this story, the quality that gives the book its distinctiveness, is not the heroism of human efforts or achievements but of trust, of "handing everything over" and relying completely on Another.

4

"Putting the Clock Back": Progress in *The Voyage of the "Dawn Treader"*

AFTER discussing the Moral Law and the power behind it, in the opening chapters of *Mere Christianity,* Lewis pauses to raise for at least some readers the protest that this is turning out to be only religion, which, after all, the world has tried already, and "you cannot put the clock back." Lewis writes in reply,

> Would you think I was joking if I said that you can put a clock back, and that if the clock is wrong it is often a very sensible thing to do? But I would rather get away from that whole idea of clocks. We all want progress. But progress means getting nearer to the place where you want to be. And if you have taken a wrong turning, then to go forward does not get you any nearer. If you are on the wrong road, progress means doing an about-turn and walking back to the right road; and in that case the man who turns back soonest is the most progressive man. ... If you look at the present state of the world, it is pretty plain that humanity has been making some big mistake. We are on the wrong road. And if that is so, we must go back. Going back is the quickest way on. (p. 36)

The third of the Chronicles of Narnia relates closely to this passage. Its plot is a series of literal and figurative "progresses," which explore simultaneously the unknown Eastern Seas and a range of social, moral, and religious concerns. Running through those progresses, unifying them, and giving them their distinctive flavor or feeling is the theme of "voyaging." It is the union of that plot and theme, of progress and voyage, that has made *The Voyage of the "Dawn Treader"* so appealing to many readers.

The story is a progress, first, as an official journey, especially of a sovereign. The *Dawn Treader,* under the leadership of King Caspian, sails east in search of the seven loyal lords who were sent off by the usurper Miraz to explore the unknown seas beyond the Lone Islands. The sense of a king on an official progress through his realm comes out particularly as Caspian enters Narrowhaven and the trumpeter cries at the castle gate, "Open for the King of Narnia, come to visit his trusty and well-beloved servant the Governor of the Lone Islands" (p. 43). The account of this progress is embodied in the traditional journey form, with its typical linear, episodic structure linked by a central character, who organizes the expedition and provides courageous leadership during it.

As a journey-narrative, *The Voyage of the "Dawn Treader"* is related to a long literary tradition. Its predecessors range from the classical voyages of Odysseus, Jason, and Aeneas, to Celtic and Germanic legends like the *Voyage of Bram* and the *Voyage of Maeldúin,* to the imaginary voyages of the seventeenth and eighteenth centuries best remembered by their satirical counterparts such as *Gulliver's Travels.* Many details in Lewis's story derive, at least ultimately, from that heritage. The voyage to scattered islands was a characteristic of the Celtic *imram,* best known by the *Voyage of St. Brendan.* The storm, with its symbolism of difficulties overcome, occurs for example in the *Odyssey* and the *Aeneid.* The gold on Deathwater Island is the temptation threatening defeat, which appears in different forms in different stories, as Circe to Odysseus and Dido to Aeneas. The Monopods are the usual encounter with exotic life forms, and the episode of the Dark Island parallels the descent to the underworld in the ancient and medieval works, which tests the hero's prowess and renews and strengthens him for the challenges to come. And the image of a paradise cut off from the world by an ocean barrier occurs frequently in the medieval journeys to Paradise.[1]

The various impediments or near defeats faced by the characters point to the broader significance of the journey tale, and to the more important link between *The Voyage of the "Dawn Treader"* and its antecedents. In its archetypal dimension, the journey has always been a tale about life as well as within life. The hero's journey also involves development in his character; it gives him experience and insight, as well as adventure. So it is with *The Voyage of the "Dawn Treader."* The journey is one of growth and maturation for the young king, who, despite his many admirable qualities, has a good deal to learn about himself and the world. When the ship reaches Felimath and the children decide to walk across the island, for example, the narrator comments, "If Caspian had been as experienced then as he became later on in this voyage he would not have made this suggestion" (pp. 30-31). He is gripped by greed on Deathwater Island and by jealousy when he learns he is not to go on to the End of the World. But in a series of episodes, he grows in wisdom, learning to rely on his mind rather than his passions. Lord Bern provides him a good example at Narrowhaven as do Reepicheep in the adventure with the sea serpent and Lucy on Deathwater Island. The final and perhaps decisive lesson is Aslan's rebuke to his surliness and quick temper near the End of the World. Caspian emerges from an encounter with Aslan in the ship's cabin a more humble and mature person: "When the others rejoined him a little later they found him changed" (p. 210). That he is ready to confront life is expressed in journey terms: "You're to go on—Reep and

Edmund, and Lucy, and Eustace; and I'm to go back" (p. 210). His journey into experience completed, Caspian is to return and marry the princess, which traditionally symbolizes maturity, readiness to encounter life as an adult. The others, having not yet completed their journeys, must travel on.

It is crucial to the story, and to Caspian's development, that the journey is a voyage. The nature of the story, the quality of the response to it, would be totally different if it were a journey by land. Partly, of course, the voyage gives to the story the peculiar flavor of the sea, as it did to Lucy when she first arrived on the *Dawn Treader:* "When they turned aft to the cabin and supper, and saw the whole western sky lit up with an immense crimson sunset, and felt the quiver of the ship, and tasted the salt on their lips, and thought of unknown lands on the eastern rim of the world, Lucy felt that she was almost too happy to speak" (p. 23). Beyond that there is the sense of mystery and excitement that oceans have always engendered: "The rest [of the old sailors] had only wild stories of islands inhabited by headless men, floating islands, waterspouts, and a fire that burned along the water" (p. 52). The voyage not only helps set the tone for the story but also shapes its archetypal qualities. It relies on two images, of a sea and a ship. The sea has traditionally symbolized the origin of life as well as a danger and threat to life. These two sides of water are reflected by the well on the top of Aslan's mountain and the name Deathwater Island, and by Caspian's reaction to the living water near the end of the voyage: "That's real water, that. I'm not sure that it isn't going to kill me. But it is the death I would have chosen" (p. 199). A ship is a traditional symbol of a microcosm, of a miniature version of the world or a community. Lewis captures this sense of compression and unity by making the *Dawn Treader* a "little bit of a thing," so small that, "forward of the mast, there was hardly any deck room between the central hatch and the ship's boat on one side and the hen-coop . . . on the other" (pp. 22, 23). A voyage, combining the images of sea and ship, is particularly well suited to the archetypal journey into experience, as the ship becomes a little world compressing the tensions and difficulties of personal and social life and forcing them upon the hero, carrying him through a symbolic journey, to encounter other difficulties and dangers and to prove his worth. Caspian, like Ulysses (to whom he is compared on page 209), Aeneas, Huckleberry Finn, and many other predecessors, is on a voyage which involves physical, emotional, and spiritual testing and maturation: he is on a progress through and beyond his kingdom, which enables him simultaneously to progress toward manhood.

Progress also appears in the book in other senses. It appears in a motif of social satire on the supposed "forward course, development" of modernism. That theme deals first with the boy who was "called Eustace Clarence Scrubb, and . . . almost deserved it" (p. 1). His parents "were very up-to-date and advanced people. They were vegetarians, non-smokers and teetotallers and wore a special kind of underclothes. In their house there was very little furniture and very few clothes on the beds and the windows were always open" (p. 1). Eustace himself is a scientist and pseudointellectual: "Eustace Clarence liked animals, especially beetles, if they were dead and pinned on a card. He liked books if they were books of information and had pictures of grain elevators or of fat foreign children doing exercises in model schools" (pp. 1-2). Eustace's own intellectual training was at a modern, if not model, school: "Eustace (of course) was at a school where they didn't have corporal punishment" (p. 28). There he developed a utilitarian attitude toward his studies: "Though he didn't care much about any subject for its own sake, he cared a great deal about marks" (p. 24). All this is summed up by Eustace's

preference for "liners and motor-boats and aeroplanes" over
the trim and graceful *Dawn Treader* (p. 23).

The satire on modernism is aimed particularly at his
Sufficiency, the Governor of the Lone Islands. Gumpas assures Caspian that the slave trade is "an essential part of
the economic development of the islands" (p. 47). When
Caspian disagrees, Gumpas replies that he has statistics
and graphs to demonstrate the economic problem involved.

> "Tender as my years may be," said Caspian, "I believe I
> understand the slave trade from within quite as well as your
> Sufficiency. And I do not see that it brings into the islands
> meat or bread or beer or wine or timber or cabbages or books
> or instruments of music or horses or armour or anything else
> worth having. But whether it does or not, it must be stopped."
> "But that would be putting the clock back," gasped the
> Governor. "Have you no idea of progress, of development?"
> "I have seen them both in an egg," said Caspian. "We call
> it *Going bad* in Narnia. This trade must stop." (pp. 47-48)

This passage echoes the words quoted above from *Mere
Christianity,*[2] and it draws in their point as well. In the
slave trade in Narnia, as in education and family life in
our world, it is pretty plain some big mistakes have been
made. The worst of those mistakes are departures from the
natural—Caspian's comments to Gumpas indicate that the
slave trade does not produce "real" or "natural" goods. Like
the practice of charging interest on money, which was forbidden for many centuries, it is condemned as an unnatural and cruel economic practice. Similarly, family life has
been undermined by unnatural practices. Eustace "didn't
call his father and mother 'Father' and 'Mother,' but Har-
old and Alberta" (p. 1). Regard for the natural distinctions
between parents and children has been lost and that, actually and symbolically, lies behind a disintegration in
family and society. We are on the wrong road; therefore,
going back to old values is the quickest way on.

A third variation on progress also involves Eustace,

whose adventure exemplifies a progress to self-awareness through "going back." From the first Eustace is disagreeable ("Deep down inside he liked bossing and bullying"— p. 2) and selfish ("Lucy gives me a little of her water ration. She says girls don't get as thirsty as boys. I had often thought this but it ought to be more generally known at sea"—p. 62). The ultimate, and most humiliating, indication of his character is the inability of the slave traders to get rid of him, even thrown "in free with other lots": "Though no one would want to be sold as a slave, it is perhaps even more galling to be a sort of utility slave whom no one will buy" (p. 51). Through his selfishness, laziness, and greed, Eustace—in a wonderfully detailed and realistic scene—discovers he has turned into a dragon. He spends several days in that state and comes to realize that all along he has been "pretty beastly" and has behaved like a "monster" (pp. 91, 76).

At that point Aslan takes him to a pool in a garden on a mountain. The water in the pool, Eustace later tells Edmund, "was as clear as anything and I thought if I could get in there and bathe it would ease the pain in my leg. But the lion told me I must undress first" (pp. 88-89). Three times Eustace peels off his dragon skin and three times it grows right back.

> "Then the lion said—but I don't know if it spoke—You will have to let me undress you. I was afraid of his claws, I can tell you, but I was pretty nearly desperate now. So I just lay flat down on my back to let him do it.
> "The very first tear he made was so deep that I thought it had gone right into my heart. And when he began pulling the skin off, it hurt worse than anything I've ever felt. . . . Well, he peeled the beastly stuff right off—just as I thought I'd done it myself the other three times, only they hadn't hurt—and there it was lying on the grass: only ever so much thicker, and darker, and more knobbly looking than the others had been. . . . Then he caught hold of me—I didn't like that much for I was very tender underneath now that I'd no skin on—

and threw me into the water. It smarted like anything but only for a moment. After that it became perfectly delicious and as soon as I started swimming and splashing I found that all the pain had gone from my arm. And then I saw why. I'd turned into a boy again. . . .

"After a bit the lion took me out and dressed me—"

"Dressed you. With his paws?"

"Well, I don't exactly remember that bit. But he did some-how or other: in new clothes—the same I've got on now, as a matter of fact. And then suddenly I was back here." (pp. 90-91)

Like the death scene of *The Lion, the Witch and the Ward-robe,* this episode is permeated with Christian ideas and symbols. The use of the number three, the inability of Eus-tace to change himself, the water into which he is plunged, and the new clothes unite to make this event the Narnian equivalent of rebirth and baptism. The archetypal over-tones of the water image reinforce the Christian meanings. The use of water to symbolize purification draws upon the inherent virtues of water as a cleansing agent. And the use of water (especially immersion into and rising out of water) is effective in symbolizing rebirth because of the traditional associations of water with death and life. This stage of Eustace's spiritual journey, then, which began as he fell into the briny waters of a picture at home, culmi-nates in the well of life on a mountain in Narnia. Eustace in Narnia, like so many persons in our world, was a rebel who must lay down his arms: "Laying down your arms, surrendering, . . . realising that you have been on the wrong track and getting ready to start life over again from the ground floor—that is the only way out of a 'hole.' This process of surrender—this movement full speed astern— is what Christians call repentance" *(Mere Christianity,* p. 59). In the words of the story, after his experience on Dragon Island Eustace "began to be a different boy" (p. 93). He had been on the wrong road, he did an about-turn and returned to the right road, and now he can begin to progress.[3]

A fourth variation on progress is that of Lucy, a progress toward maturity and toward spiritual maturity in particular. At first glance Lucy might not seem to need such growth. She is, after all, unselfish to all, generous to a fault with Eustace, and even potentially sacrificial when seeking to make the Dufflepuds visible. And, as Edmund mentions in telling Eustace about Aslan, "Lucy sees him most often" (p. 92). But Lucy, like the others, is young; she too needs to grow through experience. The central episode in Lucy's development comes at the Magician's house, especially as she looks in the Magician's Book. Several details suggest that the book, at one level, is a symbol of life. "There was," for example, "no title page or title; the spells began straight away" (p. 128). Also, "You couldn't turn back. The right-hand pages, the ones ahead, could be turned; the left hand pages could not" (p. 133). More specifically, it symbolizes Lucy's life. As Lucy gazes at a page, she sees "a picture of a girl standing at a reading-desk reading in a huge book. And the girl was dressed exactly like Lucy" (p. 129). What she sees in the book is "much more than a picture. It [is] alive" (p. 132). Within that book of life are a variety of opportunities to do good ("How to remember things forgotten"—p. 129) or evil ("How to give a man an ass's head"—p. 129); and a variety of temptations, some of which hold little or no appeal for Lucy, others which attract her and could well catch her in their "spell." It is the latter that develop her character the most. The temptations of pride and curiosity try her greatly, and she even yields to the latter, to her sorrow and loss.

But the Magician's Book is not only a book of life—of experience and temptation; it is also a Book of Life. Lucy encounters a series of pages which are more like a story than a spell. In them she reads "the loveliest story [she] ever read or ever shall read in [her] whole life" (p. 133).

She does not remember the story after she finishes, but she can recall a few details: "It was about a cup and a sword and a tree and a green hill" (p. 133). These symbols, clearly Christian, suggest that "the loveliest story" is the story of Christ. Just as myths of our world can be realities in Narnia, as for example Father Christmas and Bacchus,[4] so what is reality in our world becomes myth in Narnia.[5] To read that story is a useful part of Lucy's spiritual maturation in Narnia. But if she were to stay in Narnia, reading that story would not be enough: she would need to grow closer to God in his Narnian incarnation as Aslan. As Aslan said to Lucy in *Prince Caspian,* "Every year you grow, you will find me bigger" (p. 136), and her understanding of him as Aslan would need to grow every year as well.

For persons living in our world and reading the Narnian myths, the situation is just the reverse. The Narnian myths can be a means—but no more—of drawing us nearer to the divine realities in our world. That is made clear at the end of the voyage, when, in a scene which raises its Christian and archetypal symbolism to the level of high myth, the children see a lamb cooking fish on the sea shore.

> "Please, Lamb," said Lucy, "is this the way to Aslan's country?"
>
> "Not for you," said the Lamb. "For you the door into Aslan's country is from your own world."
>
> "What!" said Edmund. "Is there a way into Aslan's country from our world too?"
>
> "There is a way into my country from all the worlds," said the Lamb; but as he spoke his snowy white flushed into tawny gold and his size changed and he was Aslan himself, towering above them and scattering light from his mane.
>
> "Oh, Aslan," said Lucy. "Will you tell us how to get into your country from our world?"
>
> "I shall be telling you all the time," said Aslan.[6] "But I will not tell you how long or short the way will be; only that it lies across a river. But do not fear that, for I am the great

Bridge Builder. And now come; I will open the door in the sky and send you to your own land."

"Please, Aslan," said Lucy. "Before we go, will you tell us when we can come back to Narnia again? Please. And oh, do, do, do make it soon."

"Dearest," said Aslan very gently, "you and your brother will never come back to Narnia."

"Oh, *Aslan!*" said Edmund and Lucy both together in despairing voices.

"You are too old, children," said Aslan, "and you must begin to come close to your own world now."

"It isn't Narnia, you know," sobbed Lucy. "It's *you*. We shan't meet *you* there. And how can we live, never meeting you?"

"But you shall meet me, dear one," said Aslan.

"Are—are you there too, Sir?" said Edmund.

"I am," said Aslan. "But there I have another name. You must learn to know me by that name. This was the very reason why you were brought to Narnia, that by knowing me here for a little, you may know me better there." (pp. 215-16)

It is a powerfully evocative passage, full of Christian symbols (light, lamb, lion, river, door), biblical allusions (the passage as a whole alludes to John 21:4-19, and "I am" is the name revealed by Yahweh to Moses in Exodus 3:14), and archetypal symbolism (a river is a traditional symbol of death and a bridge of the passage to another world). In reading it, however, one does not tend to isolate such features and consider their individual effects: all its components unite to let the passage appeal directly to the emotion and the imagination. It contains, as great myth always does, more than the author could have intended and conveys, through story and symbols, things the author could not have put into words. For readers of the Narnian stories in our world, this episode and the other Narnian myths can be a beginning, a useful part of their spiritual growth, as Lucy's reading the story of Christ in Narnia was for her. But for them, as for Lucy, reading the myths of the other world is not enough. Further progress toward spiritual

maturity requires getting to know Aslan by his earthly
name and learning to know him as a reality in our world.

Reepicheep's adventure, the final variation on "progress," is a progress in the sense of a journey toward Aslan's
own country. All his life he has desired to reach that goal.
He tells Lucy,

> When I was in my cradle a wood woman, a Dryad, spoke
> this verse over me:
>> Where sky and water meet,
>> Where the waves grow sweet,
>> Doubt not, Reepicheep,
>> To find all you seek,
>> There is the utter East.
> I do not know what it means. But the spell of it has been
> on me all my life. (pp. 16-17)

The "spell" Reepicheep mentions seems close to the pang
of longing which haunted Lewis throughout his early life
and which he elsewhere calls "Joy": "An unsatisfied desire
which is itself more desirable than any other satisfaction."[7]
He describes that desire briefly in *Mere Christianity*:
"Probably earthly pleasures were never meant to satisfy
it, but only to arouse it, to suggest the real thing. If that
is so, . . . I must keep alive in myself the desire for my true
country . . . ; I must make it the main object of life to press
on to that other country and to help others to do the same"
(p. 120). Such longing is felt most often by persons with
romantic inclinations. It is significant, therefore, that Reepicheep is a romantic hero. He is brave—"the most valiant
of all the Talking Beasts of Narnia" (p. 11)—and idealistic:
"We did not set sail to look for things useful but to seek
honour and adventures" (p. 152). His mind is "full of for-
lorn hopes, death or glory charges, and last stands"
(pp. 55-56). He knows, as Lewis came to know eventually,
that the object he longs for is not this world but another
world. To "go on into the utter east and never return into

the world," to find unity with Aslan in his country, is his heart's desire (p. 179).

Though Reepicheep is on a pilgrimage, it is not one toward maturity: his faith in Aslan is sure, his commitment is total. The strength of that commitment makes Reepicheep, in a sense, rather than Caspian, the guiding spirit of the expedition. He is the first to approach the dragon when it lands by their camp, the one who is consulted about whether Lucy should look for the Magician's Book, and the one whose idea saves the ship from the sea serpent. It is Reepicheep who replies to the terrifying voice which comes out of the blackness near the Dark Island. His words not only inspire the rest of the crew but also are the strongest influence on the "voyaging" quality which shapes the tone of the book and lingers as its most lasting effect: "My own plans are made. While I can, I sail east in the *Dawn Treader*. When she fails me, I paddle east in my coracle. When she sinks, I shall swim east with my four paws. And when I can swim no longer, if I have not reached Aslan's country, or shot over the edge of the world in some vast cataract, I shall sink with my nose to the sunrise and Peepiceek will be head of the talking mice in Narnia" (p. 184). Reepicheep does "want acutely . . . something that cannot be had in this world" *(Mere Christianity,* p. 119) and he has committed himself completely to reaching the place where that want will be satisfied.

Perhaps it is inevitable, given his commitment and his spirit, that he should be the first to partake of the food on Aslan's Table. The table is on an island near the end of the world. "On the table itself there was set out such a banquet as had never been seen, not even when Peter the High King kept his court at Cair Paravel. There were turkeys and geese and peacocks, there were boar's heads and sides of venison, there were pies shaped like ships under full sail or like dragons and elephants, there were ice puddings and bright lobsters and gleaming salmon, there were nuts and grapes, pineapples and peaches, pomegranates and melons and tomatoes" (pp. 165-66). The table is the Narnian equivalent of the Eucharist, or Lord's Supper, of Christianity. It is a table of remembrance (the stone knife lying on it, the same one "the White Witch used when she killed Aslan at the Stone Table long ago," has been "brought here to be kept in honour while the world lasts"—p. 173) and a table of nourishment, physically (for "all were very hungry"—p. 174) and spiritually, for only those who "believe" in its goodness eat at it (p. 173). And it is a magic table, "eaten [by birds from the East], and renewed, every day" (p. 174). The table appears at the end of the voyage: "It is set here by [Aslan's] bidding . . . for those who come so far" (p. 174). It is, apparently, a reward for those who have come this far in their pilgrimage, but is also a source of strength for those who desire to journey further, to—and beyond—the very end of the world.

Reepicheep, of course, does desire to go further, and as he nears his goal, the images of sea and ship return. The sea is the Silver Sea, a body of sweet water covered with lilies, a traditional symbol of life. The ship is a coracle, "a tiny boat, barely four feet long" (p. 95), with room only for Reepicheep—in this final stage of his journey toward spiritual fulfillment, toward union with Aslan, he must "go on alone" (p. 213). The sense of "voyaging," with its peculiar overtones of romance and nostalgia, is powerful at the end of the voyage, created especially by two images always associated with "joy" for Lewis, mountains and music. As Reepicheep leaves the children to go on in his coracle and bids them good-bye, he tries to be sad for their sakes, but he quivers with happiness. "Then hastily he got into his coracle and took his paddle, and the current caught it and away he went, very black against the lilies. But no lilies grew on the wave; it was a smooth green slope. The coracle went more and more quickly, and beautifully it rushed up the wave's side. For one split second they saw its shape and Reepicheep's on the very top. Then it vanished, and since that moment no one can truly claim to have seen Reepicheep the Mouse. But my belief is that he came safe to Aslan's country and is alive there to this day" (p. 213). His progress is complete and his longing for Aslan's Country and Aslan himself has been perfectly fulfilled.

In an essay written in 1958 Lewis asks "Is Progress Possible?"[8] The answer is that in the social areas the essay is considering, progress may be possible, but only at the cost of personal freedom. Spiritual progress, however, is a different matter. Lewis wrote in *Mere Christianity,* "There are three things that spread the Christ life to us: baptism, belief, and that mysterious action which different Christians call by different names—Holy Communion, the Mass, the Lord's Supper" (p. 62). The Narnian equivalents for these, reinforced by a sense of longing for spiritual fulfillment, influence the different spiritual journeys of Caspian, Eustace, Lucy, and Reepicheep in *The Voyage of the "Dawn Treader."* Starting at different points, arriving by the end of the story at different levels, they illustrate that in the spiritual realm, in contrast to the social, progress is possible and that it invariably involves retreat. Going back to find the right road is not just the quickest, but the only way on.

5

"You Must Use the Map": Signs and Scripture in *The Silver Chair*

NORTHROP Frye, in *The Secular Scripture,* describes four primary narrative movements in literature: "First, the descent from a higher world; second, the descent to a lower world; third, the ascent from a lower world; and fourth, the ascent to a higher world. All stories in literature are complications of, or metaphorical derivations from, these four narrative radicals."[1] This pattern mirrors, or perhaps grew out of, experiences from many areas of human life. It reflects the structure of the universe assumed to be true until the nineteenth century, of—in descending order—Olympus or heaven, earth, and hell or hades. It relates to the human cycle of descent to this world at birth, further descent at death, and ascent after death or at a later resurrection. And it is at the heart of Christianity, as the words of the Apostle's Creed bring out nicely: Christ was "born of the Virgin Mary; suffered under Pontius Pilate, was crucified, dead, and buried; he descended into hell; the third day he rose again from the dead; he ascended into heaven, and sitteth on the right hand of God the Father Almighty." One of the basic appeals of *The Silver Chair,* the fourth volume in the Chronicles of Narnia, one way in which it rings true and conveys its meanings, is that it incorporates, consecutively, all four of these movements into its structure and meaning.

Its structure and meaning are also shaped by a repeated use of water imagery. The children float into Narnia above the sea, and King Caspian sails away and returns on the sea. The children and Puddleglum are taken across a subterranean ocean as they search for Rilian, and are threatened by a rising underland flood as they escape with Rilian. But the most important of the water images occurs already in the second chapter. Jill Pole, after leaving our world with Eustace Scrubb and seeing Eustace fall over an enormously high cliff, has a long cry and then finds herself "dreadfully thirsty" (p. 15). Hearing a stream nearby, she goes toward it but finds, lying in her path, a lion who says to her, "If you are thirsty, come and drink" (p. 16). His invitation, which alludes to Christ's words in the New Testament, "If any man thirst, let him come unto me, and drink" (John 7:37), draws into *The Silver Chair* the significance of water in the Gospel of John and particularly in the episode of the Samaritan woman. When she met Christ at Jacob's well, where she had come to fill her pitcher with water, he offered her spiritual water instead: "Whosoever drinketh of the water that I shall give him shall never thirst; but the water that I shall give him shall be in him a well of water springing up into everlasting life" (John 4:14). When the woman receives and believes Christ's words, her spiritual thirst is quenched; she takes those words to her friends, who also believe; and she brings other persons to listen to Christ and they believe also, "because of his own word" (4:41). The episode illustrates what Christ affirmed a bit later, "The words that I speak unto you, they are spirit, and they are life" (6:63).

The words spoken by Christ in our world are parallel to words spoken to Jill by Aslan soon after her arrival in Narnia. After Jill drinks from the stream and satisfies her thirst, Aslan gives four signs to help her and Eustace find the lost Prince Rilian, the task for which Aslan called them into Narnia:

> These are the Signs by which I will guide you in your quest. First; as soon as the Boy Eustace sets foot in Narnia, he will meet an old and dear friend. He must greet that friend at once; if he does, you will both have good help. Second; you must journey out of Narnia to the north till you come to the ruined city of the ancient giants. Third; you shall find a writing on a stone in that ruined city, and you must do what the writing tells you. Fourth; you will know the lost Prince (if you find him) by this, that he will be the first person you have met in your travels who will ask you to do something in my name, in the name of Aslan. (pp. 19-20)

Aslan then directs her to "remember, remember, remember the Signs. Say them to yourself when you wake in the morning and when you lie down at night, and when you wake in the middle of the night" (p. 21). These lines also contain a biblical allusion, to Moses's words as he delivered the law to the children of Israel (Deut. 6:6-7). The signs become for Jill, like the words of the law or the words of Christ in our world, a source of direction and guidance. The image of the signs in Narnia resembles quite closely the comparison of theology to a map in *Mere Christianity:* "Doctrines are not God: they are only a kind of map. But that map is based on the experience of hundreds of people who really were in touch with God" (p. 136). And Lewis urges his readers to hold some of the main doctrines of Christianity "before your mind for some time every day. That is why daily prayers and religious reading and churchgoing are necessary parts of the Christian life. We have to be continually reminded of what we believe" (p. 124). The message for Jill and for Christians in our world is the same, "If you want to get any further, you must use the map" (p. 136).

Although in this case the idea to be imaged is introduced early, it is quickly subordinated to the story, that of

Jill and Eustace's search for the lost Prince Rilian. Because the story, as a journey and as a search, is the most nearly pure romance of the Narnia books, the archetypal significances inherent in that form can be helpful in better understanding its structure and themes. Its narrative pattern, the most basic of romance forms, is emphasized by use of the word "quest" (pp. 19, 199) and by the references to the "task" the children are to perform: "I lay on you this command, that you seek this lost Prince until either you have found him and brought him to his father's house, or else died in the attempt, or else gone back into your own world" (p. 19; also p. 18). Lewis complicates the structure by including a second quest, a quest within a quest: there is the children's search for Prince Rilian who disappeared ten years before, but Prince Rilian, when he disappeared, was himself on a quest, seeking revenge for the death of his mother. The story uses character types typical of romance—a brave prince, a wise older guide, an evil witch; typical romance motifs—the lost child, the dangerous journey, a symbolic death and rebirth; and the basic romance structure—separation (Chapters 3-5), ordeal (Chapters 6-12), and return (Chapters 13-16). As the romance structure combines with the idea of the Word, as the signs which give guidance combine with the downward and upward movement of the romance form and the vertical movement of the quest, structure and theme unite to achieve the distinctive quality and meaning of the book.

The first stage of the descent is from the cliff into Narnia: Eustace falls over the cliff when he tries to rescue Jill, who had been showing off, and Jill follows later when Aslan, who gave Eustace a safe ride down, sends her down on his breath as well. Because Eustace does not know what Aslan told Jill and does not recognize the doddering old king as his friend Caspian, they quickly muff the first sign. But they receive help from Glimfeather and his folk at a Parliament of Owls, who fill in the background for the story. While out maying in the north parts of Narnia, the Queen, Caspian's wife, was bitten and killed by a great green serpent, which Prince Rilian pursued but could not apprehend. Thereafter Rilian spent his days riding the northern marches, "hunting for that venomous worm, to kill it and be avenged" (p. 50). But he soon mentioned to Lord Drinian that he encountered, by the fountain where his mother was killed, "the most beautiful lady he had ever seen" (p. 51), who beckoned for the prince to join her. A few days later, Prince Rilian rode out again "and from that hour no trace of him was ever found in Narnia nor any neighbouring land" (p. 51).

That a mother is killed while maying provides significant clues to the nature of the Witch and to the archetypal meanings involved in the episode. The Witch is an evil temptress, another Circe figure: the wise owls recognize her similarity to the same type of figure in *The Lion, the Witch and the Wardrobe:* "Long, long ago, at the very beginning, a White Witch came out of the North and bound our land in snow and ice for a hundred years. And we think this may be one of the same crew" (p. 52).[2] Although, when Drinian sees her, she is wearing a thin garment "as green as poison" and although it strikes him that "this shining green woman was evil" (p. 51), she is not Satan or a devil-figure. She is the figure of evil in this fairy story, but that evil is handled in the manner of romance, not theology. In keeping with her place in the Circe tradition, she dislikes motherhood, creativity, and men. Thus, on the holiday which celebrates the return of growth and fertility, she kills a mother and makes plans to entice and enslave a sterling example of young manhood. Rilian's mother, the daugher of a star, recognizes the nature of her attacker and tries to warn her son of his danger: "As long as the life was in her she seemed to be trying hard to tell him something. But she could not speak clearly and, whatever her message was, she died without delivering it" (p. 49).

The Witch's hatred goes beyond the royal family to the nation itself: "She has some use for him, and some deep scheme against Narnia," the owls conclude (p. 52). There lingers on in her the animosity the White Witch felt toward Narnia as a place of life, beauty, and freedom.[3] She plans, therefore, to rule the Narnians through Rilian, who will murder their natural lords and hold "their throne as a bloody and foreign tyrant" (p. 150). The archetypal nature of the Witch is made particularly clear by the words of the oldest Dwarf: "Those Northern Witches always mean the same thing, but in every age they have a different plan for getting it" (p. 201).

The separation stage of the children's quest occurs shortly afterward on the northern edge of Narnia. The owls have transported Jill and Eustace as far as the Marsh-wiggles, where they are entrusted to Puddleglum, one of Lewis's most fascinating characters. A tall, skinny, frog-like creature, Puddleglum is able to find a dark lining to even the brightest of clouds. " 'Good morning, Guests,' it said. 'Though when I say *good* I don't mean it won't probably turn to rain or it might be snow, or fog, or thunder. You didn't get any sleep, I dare say' " (p. 58). With Puddleglum as companion and guide, the children set out across Ettinsmoor in search of the ruined city mentioned in the second sign: "It stands to reason we're not likely to get very far on a journey to the North, not at this time of the year, with the winter coming on soon and all. And an early winter too, by the look of things. But you mustn't let that make you downhearted. Very likely, what with enemies, and mountains, and rivers to cross, and losing our way, and next to nothing to eat, and sore feet, we'll hardly notice the weather" (p. 61).

All those difficulties they are able to cope with, however, as they travel northward past the giants and across the moor, and reach an ancient bridge spanning a deep ravine. When they cross the bridge, they meet their first

serious danger, an internal threat. A beautiful lady dressed
in a long, fluttering dress of dazzling green, riding with a
knight in black armor, advises them to stop for the winter,
or for a rest, with the gentle giants at the castle of Harfang.
"There you shall have steaming baths, soft beds, and bright
hearts; and the roast and the baked and the sweet and the
strong will be on the table four times in a day" (p. 76). Her
words do to them what the weather, roads, and giants were
not able to: "Whatever the Lady had intended by telling
them about Harfang, the actual effect on the children was
a bad one. They could think about nothing but beds and
baths and hot meals and how lovely it would be to get
indoors. They never talked about Aslan, or even about the
lost Prince, now. And Jill gave up her habit of repeating
the Signs over to herself every night and morning. She
said to herself, at first, that she was too tired, but she soon
forgot all about it" (pp. 79-80). By yielding to the temptation of relaxation, of decreased vigilance, they miss the
second sign, even as they stumble across the squares and
oblongs of the ruined city on a flat hilltop, and the third
sign, although Jill falls into one of its letters. Instead of
concentrating on Aslan's signs, they have begun to think
of themselves and to rely on their own judgment. They
have put themselves into the hands of symbolic giants, of
emotional forces which could devour them, even before they
walk into the hands of the literal giants at Harfang. Puddleglum tries to get them to stop, review the signs, and
look around them, but the children can think only "of baths
and beds and hot drinks; and the idea of coming to Harfang
too late and being shut out was almost unbearable" (p. 89).

In a sense, then, the internal threat Harfang poses is
a greater danger than the physical threat, though the latter is great enough: the Gentle Giants come very close to
literally *having* the travelers "for [their] Autumn Feast,"
as the second meaning of Eustace's words put it (p. 95).
Fortunately the travelers escape through an open pantry

door, during the cook's nap, and the giant King's fears are realized: "We'll have no man-pies to-morrow" (p. 117). Meantime, they have had to confront the inner threat as well. Jill, during their night at Harfang, dreams of a lion, who "told her to repeat the Signs, and she found that she had forgotten them all. At that, a great horror came over her." As the dream continues, the lion shows Jill, through the window, "written in great letters across the world or the sky (she did not know which) . . . the words UNDER ME" (p. 100). The words, which anticipate those they will see next day cut in the pavement of the City Ruinous, at this point are another sign—an affirmation of power and authority which should strengthen them now and in the future stages of their ordeal. Puddleglum, later, in the palace of the Queen of Deep Realm, gives overt expression to what the words at this point imply: "There *are* no accidents. Our guide is Aslan; and he was there when the giant king caused the letters to be cut, and he knew already all things that would come of them" (p. 134). Next morning, the children look out a window of the palace and see, "spread out like a map," the second sign, "the ruins of a gigantic city" (p. 101). And across the center of the city is the third sign, "in large, dark lettering . . . the words UNDER ME" (p. 102). The travelers now must begin again to rely on the signs, to trust in their guide, to follow the "map" they have been given in order to find the Prince and to meet the threats which are still to come when they do.

After the travellers slip out of the Castle of Harfang and escape from the giants by crawling through a slight crevice between the huge rocks, they slide down a long gravelly incline in what becomes the second stage of their descent. The characteristics Frye gives for the descent are particularly pertinent here:

> The general theme of descent . . . [is] that of a growing confusion of identity and of restrictions on action. There is a

72

break in consciousness at the beginning, with analogies to falling asleep, followed by a descent to a lower world which is sometimes a world of cruelty and imprisonment. . . . In the descent there is a growing isolation and immobility: charms and spells hold one motionless; human beings are turned into subhuman creatures, and made more mechanical in behavior; hero or heroine are trapped in labyrinths or prisons. (*The Secular Scripture,* p. 129)

This level of descent is usually the greatest test of one's character, as it images the descent into the depths of despair, the pilgrimage into the dark night of the soul, which must either crush the spirit or force it to rise from the worst with new strength and courage.

The characteristics described by Frye appear in Lewis's underworld, though with the complication that, since two quests are under way, the characteristics are divided between them. The underworld ordeal of Jill, Eustace, and Puddleglum is characterized by sleep, isolation, and immobility and ties back to the dangers they faced on the plains before they reached Harfang. After being captured by a company of gnomes, they can reassure themselves, as they are led on a long journey through cavern after cavern and a lengthy voyage over an underland sea, that, in Puddleglum's words, "We're back on the right lines. We were to go under the Ruined City, and we *are* under it. We're following the instructions again" (p. 128). As they reach the underworld city, meet the Black Knight, and stand watch during his nighttime "enchantment," they must continue to follow instructions. They have resolved not to be influenced by the Prince's pleas while he is "enchanted" and they are able to remain "steady" even when the Prince says, loud and clear, "Quick! I am sane now. Every night I am sane. If only I could get out of this enchanted chair, it would last. I should be a man again" (p. 143). And when the fourth sign appears, they have no trouble recognizing it:

"Once and for all," said the prisoner, "I adjure you to set me free. By all fears and all loves, by the bright skies of Overland, by the great Lion, by Aslan himself, I charge you—"

"Oh!" cried the three travellers as though they had been hurt. "It's the Sign," said Puddleglum. "It was the *words* of the Sign," said Scrubb more cautiously. "Oh, what *are* we to do?" said Jill. (p. 145)

Their real difficulty, now, is to remember and follow the sign given them at the Castle of Harfang, that everything is "UNDER ME." They wonder, for example, if the reference to Aslan is not a mere accident. But, they must remember, as Puddleglum had said but an hour or so before, that "there *are* no accidents." And it is Puddleglum again who puts the proper emphasis on trust:

"Oh, if only we knew!" said Jill.

"I think we do know," said Puddleglum.

"Do you mean you think everything will come right if we do untie him?" said Scrubb.

"I don't know about that," said Puddleglum. "You see, Aslan didn't tell Pole what would happen. He only told her what to do. That fellow will be the death of us once he's up, I shouldn't wonder. But that doesn't let us off following the Sign." (p. 146)

They do trust, they do follow the sign, and for the moment everything does come right. Half of the children's quest has been achieved; having been "sent by Aslan himself from beyond the world's end to seek your Highness" (p. 147), they have found him. Now they must escape with him and bring him back to his father's house.

Rilian's ordeal reflects Frye's images of imprisonment, immobility, reduction to subhumanness, and confused consciousness. It focuses on the traditional quest theme of identity, as a hero, having gone out from home, demonstrates his strength and maturity by surviving his ordeal and returning to a life of usefulness. The ordeal forces him to question his identity and leads him to find, or regain, it. By yielding to the Witch's temptation to follow her, Rilian loses touch with reality. He is deceived about the Witch: "She is a nosegay of all virtues, as truth, mercy, constancy, gentleness, courage and the rest. I say what I know. Her kindness to me alone, who can in no way reward her, would make an admirable history" (p. 132). And he is deceived about his own identity: "How do you call him?—Billian? Trillian? in my Lady's realm. Indeed, to my certain knowledge, there is no such man here" (p. 133). His behavior indeed becomes mechanical—his enchantment makes him "the toy and lap-dog, nay, more likely the pawn and tool, of the most devilish sorceress that ever planned the woe of men" (p. 144). The gnomes, who are also turned into subhuman, or subgnomian, creatures by the Witch's enchantments, state the theme nicely after the Witch's death releases them: "We didn't know who we were or where we belonged. We couldn't do anything, or think anything, except what she put into our heads" (p. 177). Only after the others free Rilian from his enchantment and imprisonment, can he affirm that "I know myself. ... I am the King's son of Narnia, Rilian, the only child of Caspian, Tenth of that name, whom some call Caspian the Seafarer" (p. 151). As he reflects back on what he has escaped, he sums up the experience: "For now that I am myself I can remember that enchanted life, though while I was enchanted I could not remember my true self" (p. 148).

Although the Prince has recovered his identity, his quest has not yet been fulfilled and all four must face another test of consciousness and alertness. When the Witch returns a bit later, she begins to work an enchantment by incense and hypnotic music. The sweet smell and the thrumming sound confuse their minds as the Witch says again and again that the overworld is but a dream, a figment of imagination: "There never was any world but mine" (p. 154). As on the plains outside of Harfang, the temptation is to cease being vigilant and to forget the signs, in

this case the signs of reality. Puddleglum, fighting hard
against the enchantment, recalls them: "I've seen the sky
full of stars. I've seen the sun coming up out of the sea of
a morning and sinking behind the mountains at night"
(p. 154), and they testify to the reality of the overworld
and of its maker. The words of the previous night's dream
should serve as a new sign: the world and even the underworld are under Aslan; and Jill, with a great effort, re-
members: "There's Aslan" (p. 156). But the Witch's reply
nearly overwhelms their vigilance with relaxation and
comfort: " 'Tis a pretty make-believe. . . . There is no Narnia, no Overworld, no sky, no sun, no Aslan. And now, to
bed all. . . . To bed; to sleep; deep sleep, soft pillows, sleep
without foolish dreams" (p. 157). They are saved from the
enchantment by Puddleglum, who uses the discomfort and
pain of stamping out the fire to clear his head and to affirm
his faith in the "signs": "Suppose we *have* only dreamed,
or made up, all those things—trees and grass and sun and
moon and stars and Aslan himself. Suppose we have. Then
all I can say is that, in that case, the made-up things seem
a good deal more important than the real ones. . . . I'm
going to live as like a Narnian as I can even if there isn't
any Narnia" (p. 159). At that the Witch transforms herself
into the serpent form in which she attacked Rilian's mother
and, as the others combine their efforts to kill her, the
objectives of both quests are achieved: Rilian's "royal
mother is avenged" and Rilian is freed from being "the
slave of my mother's slayer" (p. 161).

Having completed their ordeal, having undergone a
symbolic death and been given new life, the characters
have completed the descent stages of their journey. The
themes and images of ascent reverse those of descent and,
in Frye's words, "the chief conceptions are those of escape,
remembrance, or discovery of one's real identity, growing
freedom, and the breaking of enchantment" (*The Secular
Scripture,* p. 129). The words of Glog, one of the gnomes

freed from enchantment when the Witch died, sum up those images: "You see, we're all poor gnomes from Bism whom the Witch has called up here by magic to work for her. But we'd forgotten all about it till that crash came and the spell broke. . . . I've nearly forgotten how to make a joke or dance a jig. But the moment the bang came and the chasm opened and the sea began rising, it all came back" (p. 177). Ironically, the gnomes' ascent is downward, into the dazzling, rich, secure land of Bism: "We all set off as quick as we could to get down the crack and home to our own place."

To the overworlders, ascent is less simple and sure, but again they are given a sign. Rilian's shield, which hitherto was black and without a device, now turns bright as silver and on it appears the figure of a lion: " 'Doubtless,' said the Prince. 'This signifies that Aslan will be our good lord, whether he means us to live or die. And all's one, for that' " (p. 168). Their ability to accept that sign, to trust in Aslan as they begin "the slow, weary march uphill" (p. 184) and find themselves eventually in utter darkness, illustrates the extent to which they have, through their ordeal, come to know themselves and to trust in Another. The first stage of their ascent is complete when they realize that "they [have] not only got out into the Upper World at last, but [have] come out in the heart of Narnia" (p. 192). They arrive on the evening of the Great Snow Dance:

> A lot of people were moving about, . . . trim little fauns, and dryads with leaf-crowned hair floating behind them. . . . Then [Jill] saw that they were really doing a dance—a dance with so many complicated steps and figures that it took you some time to understand it. . . . Circling round and round the dancers was a ring of Dwarfs, all dressed in their finest clothes; mostly scarlet with fur-lined hoods and golden tassles and big furry top-boots. As they circled round they were all diligently throwing snowballs. . . . They weren't throwing them *at* the dancers as silly boys might have been doing in England. They were throwing them through the dance in such perfect time

with the music and with such perfect aim that if all the dancers were in exactly the right places at exactly the right moments, no one would be hit. (pp. 192-93)

It is fitting that, at the end of a quest which required following directions and full trust in their giver, the heroes and heroine are greeted by a dance which, in its complex pattern and need for complete cooperation, symbolizes such adherence and trust.

The structure of the romance, Frye notes, is circular: "Most romances exhibit a cyclical movement of descent into a night world and a return to the idyllic world, or to some symbol of it like a marriage" (*The Secular Scripture,* p. 54). Symmetry is achieved in *The Silver Chair* first by a return to Cair Paravel, where King Caspian, who was departing in Chapter 3, returns in Chapter 16. A tone of celebration is conveyed by "solemn, triumphal music" in the background. But Lewis replaces the traditional marriage of the prince with the death of the king:

> They could see King Caspian raising his hand to bless his son. And everyone cheered, but it was a half-hearted cheer, for they all felt that something was going wrong. Then suddenly the King's head fell back upon his pillows, the Musicians stopped and there was a dead silence. The Prince, kneeling by the King's bed, laid down his head upon it and wept. . . . And after that . . . the music began again: this time, a tune to break your heart. (pp. 209-10)

It is conventional for a romance, however, to have a happy, not a heartbreaking, conclusion. Such an ending is achieved by the second phase of ascent, the return to Aslan's Mountain, which completes the circular structure of the story. When Aslan tells the children he has come "to bring [them] Home" (p. 210), his words apply to King Caspian as well, for he too has ascended to Aslan's Mountain, where "all three stood and wept" over his body (p. 211). Christian imagery confirms the theme already anticipated by the ro-

mance structure, that death is not something to be feared
or regretted. That imagery begins with water: the King's
body lies in the same stream from which Jill drank living
water in Chapter 2. Aslan's blood is joined, significantly,
with water to symbolize new life: "The dead King began
to be changed. His white beard turned to grey, and from
grey to yellow, and got shorter and vanished altogether;
and his sunken cheeks grew round and fresh, and the wrin-
kles were smoothed, and his eyes opened, and his eyes and
lips both laughed, and suddenly he leaped up and stood
before them—a very young man, or a boy" (p. 212). The
depiction of a new life of youth and vigor in another country, of the reversal of youth's normal decline into age, provides for children (as well as adults) a beautiful picture of
death: it makes death less fearful and unnatural, for, after
all, as Aslan tells Eustace, "most people have [died], you
know" (p. 213). And the rebirth completes the movement
of the romance, as Caspian, having descended in death,
ascends to live forever in the idyllic world of Aslan's
Country.

The movements of descent and ascent which give structure to the story as a whole and provide a suitable vehicle
for the themes of revenge and rescue, of words and signs,
of identity and instruction, appear also, in a reversed image, in the frame story at Experiment House. At the beginning of the story, Jill and Eustace scramble up "the
steep, earthy slope" (p. 8) to escape the persecution of the
likes of Adela Pennyfather, Cholmondely Major, Edith
Winterblott, "Spotty" Sorner, big Bannister, and the two
loathsome Garrett twins. At the end of the story, Jill,
Eustace, and Rilian rush down the same slope, weapons in
hand, to chastize the gang (pp. 214-15). Here is reflected,
in a much milder way, the same themes as in the quest
story, for "from that day forth things changed for the better
at Experiment House" and "it became quite a good school"
(p. 216). The themes which seem distant and abstract in

the romance world of Rilian and underworld, are brought close and made real in the frame events, for Aslan "seemed to know [all about Experiment House] quite as well as they did" (p. 214), and, by logical extension, he knows other things in our world as well and gives the same assurance he gave in Narnia, that all things are UNDER HIM.

6

"Throwing Up the Sponge": Trust vs. Luck in *The Horse and His Boy*

*I*N *The Educated Imagination* Northrop Frye writes that "if you open the Bible, you'll soon come to the story of the finding of the infant Moses by Pharaoh's daughter. That's a conventional type of story, the mysterious birth of the hero. . . . It was told of Perseus in Greek legend; then it passed into literature with Euripides' play *Ion;* then it was used by Plautus and Terence and other writers of comedies; then it became a device in fiction, used in *Tom Jones* and *Oliver Twist,* and it's still going strong" (p. 42). The device, still strong and healthy, is used as the initiating incident of the fifth book of the Chronicles of Narnia. It is a device closely associated with the theme of self-knowledge. The hero does not know who he is—his initial sense of identity is incorrect—and his story concerns his efforts to discover, or regain, his true identity. Supported by the devices of the "missing twin" and of the return to one's homeland, the "lost child" device establishes the structure of *The Horse and His Boy* and its theme, a central theme in all literature, "the loss and regaining of identity" (*The Educated Imagination,* p. 55).

The "lost child" motif, in which a child is separated from his or her parents by being sold, kidnapped, or put

away and later reunited with them, is one of the most
frequently used plot situations in literature. Frye goes so
far as to call it "not *a* good plot but *the* good plot" (*The
Secular Scripture,* p. 102). One can recall, in literature,
such examples as the biblical story of Joseph (with which
Shasta's story has several affinities), *Oedipus the King,
Cymbeline, Joseph Andrews,* and many, many plays and
novels of the Victorian era. *The Horse and His Boy* opens
with that motif. As Shasta, the boy, eavesdrops on a
stranger's conversation with the man he calls Father, he
discovers that he is not the son of Arsheesh, as he has
always supposed: "This boy is manifestly no son of yours,
for your cheek is as dark as mine but the boy is fair and
white like the accursed but beautiful barbarians who in-
habit the remote north" (p. 5). And Arsheesh admits that
he discovered the boy as a baby years ago in a boat that
washed ashore and that he has no idea who the boy's parents are. The impact of this plot device derives particularly
from its exploration of the question of identity, the natural
and universal need in all people, even those whose par-
entage is known, to learn who they are. The question of
identity becomes a strong theme in *The Horse and His
Boy*—Shasta responds to the discovery that Arsheesh is
not his father, "Why, I might be anyone! . . . I might be the
son of a Tarkaan myself—or the son of the Tisroc (may he
live for ever)—or of a god!" (p. 7).

That motif blends very naturally into the quest for one's
homeland, introduced by the horse, Bree, with whom Shasta
escapes from his home and Calormen. Bree ran away from
Narnia as a foal, was captured and forced to work like an
ordinary horse, and has been longing to return home ever
since. This too is an archetypal theme, one which has reflected human desires and needs throughout the centuries.
Poets of all times have written about people's concern with
their origins, with the community in which they were born,
with a place that gives them a sense of their beginning

and thus helps give them a sense of identity. This urge was especially deep among the ancients: the greatest of the ancient stories is about Odysseus's longing to return to Ithaca. Ithaca was a rocky island on which horses could not run, few crops could be grown, and life was demanding and difficult, but it was Odysseus's homeland and the urge to return to it became a driving passion. A similar longing for their homeland is exhibited by the Israelites during their captivity: "By the rivers of Babylon, there we sat down, yea, we wept, when we remembered Zion. . . . There they that carried us away captive required of us a song. . . . How shall we sing the Lord's song in a strange land? If I forget thee, O Jerusalem, let my right hand forget her cunning. If I do not remember thee, let my tongue cleave to the roof of my mouth; if I prefer not Jerusalem above my chief joy" (Ps. 137:1-6). That concern has reappeared in a major way in the 1970s. It is reflected in the popularity of Alex Haley's *Roots,* in the growing interest in genealogical studies, and in the increasing numbers of people who visit the lands from which their forefathers emigrated.

For Lewis this natural longing for home reflects a more than natural origin. It suggests, and *The Horse and His Boy* images, the longing a soul has for its real, heavenly home. In his sermon "The Weight of Glory" Lewis discusses this "desire for our own far-off country";[1] in *Mere Christianity* he calls it "the desire for my true country, which I shall not find till after death" (p. 120). This deeper dimension of the search for one's home and thus for one's identity is conveyed by the symbolism of the North. Shasta from the first is "very interested in everything that lay to the north" (p. 2) and he says, "I've been longing to go to the north all my life" (p. 12). Bree cries out frequently, "Narnia and the North" (p. 16), a phrase which Lewis first planned to use as title for the book, and he speaks of the North in paradisal terms: " 'The happy land of Narnia—Narnia of the heathery mountains and the thymy downs, Narnia of the many rivers, the plashing glens, the mossy caverns and the deep forests ringing with hammers of the Dwarfs. Oh the sweet air of Narnia! An hour's life there is better than a thousand years in Calormen.' It ended with a whinny that sounded very like a sigh" (p. 9). The North was a source of longing for Lewis himself. When he first saw the title *Siegfried and the Twilight of the Gods,* he recalls in *Surprised by Joy,* "pure 'Northernness' engulfed me," and the longing he felt for the first time in years was like "returning at last from exile and desert lands to my own country."[2]

He develops the longing for the North by associating it and Narnia with the archetypal images of lushness and rural life, in contrast to the images of a desert and a city. A desert, though it can be a place of rugged beauty, is usually associated in people's minds with barrenness and death. So it is in *The Horse and His Boy.* When Shasta reaches the desert, "it was like coming to the end of the world for all the grass stopped quite suddenly a few feet before him and the sand began: endless level sand like on a sea shore but a bit rougher because it was never wet" (pp. 79-80). Later, when Shasta and his companions are in the middle of the desert at dawn and Shasta slowly, very slowly could see the vast grey flatness on every side, "it looked absolutely dead, like something in a dead world" (p. 123). Symbolic of that death is the absence of birds, which are mentioned repeatedly in the book: "It was the morning at last, but without a single bird to sing about it" (p. 124). The city, Tashbaan, is described earlier in the book as crowded and stifling, full of the smells of "unwashed people, unwashed dogs, scent, garlic, onions, and the piles of refuse which lay everywhere" (p. 52). Most of all, it is repressive: "In Tashbaan there is only one traffic regulation, which is that everyone who is less important has to get out of the way for everyone who is more important" (p. 53). In striking contrast, as Shasta and his fellow travelers reach the end of the desert and the beginning of the North, they find water and life: "There was soft grass on both sides of the river, and beyond the grass, trees and bushes sloped up to the bases of the cliffs. There must have been some wonderful flowering shrubs hidden in that shadowy undergrowth for the whole glade was full of the coolest, and most delicious smells. And out of the darkest recess among the trees there came a sound Shasta had never heard before—a nightingale" (p. 129). In contrast to the denseness in Tashbaan, the North is "all open park-like country with no roads or houses in sight" (p. 134). Most important, instead of the repression of Tashbaan, in the North there is freedom. "Every morning the sun is darkened in my eyes," says the Tisroc to his son, "and every night my sleep is the less refreshing, because I remember that Narnia is still free" (p. 110). The contrasting images are summed up as Aravis is leaving Tashbaan: "The air was fresh and cool and as she drew near the further bank she heard the hooting of an owl. 'Ah! That's better!' thought Aravis. She had always lived in the country and had hated every minute of her time in Tashbaan" (pp. 120-21).

Shasta and Bree, two "long-lost captive[s] returning to home and freedom" (p. 202), set off on a journey, a traditional image for growth in experience. The two in their journey present contrasting but complementary patterns: Shasta must become more adult, Bree more childlike. Shasta's journey begins in the ignorance of childhood. He is unfamiliar with the world beyond the limited horizons of the fisherman's hut—he knows nothing of geography, he has not acquired manners, he is ignorant of customs among the wealthy, he has "no notion of what a great city would be like and it frightened him" (p. 46). His awkwardness is the more pronounced because it is in constant contrast to the adult confidence of Bree which is born of broad knowledge of himself and the world. As a free-born Narnian and a trained, experienced war horse, he distinguishes himself from the simple, dumb creatures he has lived among. Bree's superior opinion of himself is manifest in the patronizing attitude which he adopts toward Shasta, as, for example, when the boy is struggling to climb onto his back for the first time: "Funny to think of me who has led cavalry charges and won races having a potato-sack like you in the saddle" (p. 14). Shasta has no reason for such self-confidence. He has always assumed himself to be the son, and little better than the slave, of a humble fisherman, who in turn was little better than a slave to his social superiors. Unlike Bree he has no reason to be proud of what he is and no basis for knowing who he is.

Bree and Shasta are joined in their journey by two female characters, also on a journey to find a homeland and new identity. Hwin, the horse, and Aravis, her girl, contrast to each other and to their respective male counterparts. In this case the human possesses self-confidence and needs to learn humility, while the horse needs to gain in self-esteem and assurance. As their journey together begins, Hwin feels "rather shy before a great war horse like Bree" and she says very little (pp. 41-42). Not so with Aravis, who is after all a Tarkheena—cultured, sophisticated, and intelligent—and converses with the assurance her social position and experience have given her: "Now it was Bree and Aravis who did nearly all the talking. Bree had lived a long time in Calormen and had always been among Tarkaans and Tarkaans' horses, and so of course he knew a great many of the same people and places that Aravis knew" (p. 41). To Shasta, however, "Aravis never spoke . . . at all if she could help it" (p. 42). Her haughtiness and self-centeredness, which place her in contrast to both Shasta and Hwin, appear especially in her attitude toward the servant she drugged in order to slip away from her home:

> "And what happened to the girl—the one you drugged?" asked Shasta.
>
> "Doubtless she was beaten for sleeping late," said Aravis

coolly. "But she was a tool and spy of my stepmother's. I am very glad they should beat her."

"I say, that was hardly fair," said Shasta.

"I did not do any of these things for the sake of pleasing *you,*" said Aravis. (p. 40)

Her attitude is summed up a bit later when Bree has to urge her to "droop [her] shoulders a bit and step heavier and try to look less like a princess" (p. 50), a problem Hwin and Shasta do not face at all.

As the four characters proceed on their journey, they pass through testing grounds which lead to self-understanding and growth—Shasta and Aravis in the city (Chapters 3-8), Bree and Hwin in the desert (Chapters 9-11). In the city of Tashbaan Shasta and Aravis encounter models which prove instrumental in their development. Shasta's model is a positive one, of what he can and would like to be, a group of men very different from the people he has lived with all his life:

> They were all as fair-skinned as himself, and most of them had fair hair. And they were not dressed like men of Calormen. Most of them had legs bare to the knee. Their tunics were of fine, bright, hardy colours—woodland green, or gay yellow, or fresh blue. Instead of turbans they wore steel or silver caps, some of them set with jewels, and one with little wings on each side of it. A few were bare-headed. The swords at their sides were long and straight, not curved like Calormene scimitars. And instead of being grave and mysterious like most Calormenes, they walked with a swing and let their arms and shoulders go free, and chatted and laughed. One was whistling. You could see that they were ready to be friends with anyone who was friendly and didn't give a fig for anyone who wasn't. Shasta thought he had never seen anything so lovely in his life. (pp. 54-55)

When Shasta is "mistaken for a prince of Archenland, wherever that is" (p. 59), and taken to the palace where the Narnians are staying, he gets to know them as "the very nicest kind of grown-up[s]" (p. 57). Although he "would

have liked to make a good impression" (p. 57), he with-
draws and stays silent, the way his life in Calormen has
taught him ("Having been brought up by a hard, close-fisted
man like Arsheesh, he had a fixed habit of never telling
grown-ups anything if he could help it"—p. 70); and because he is in the room as the Narnians discuss their strat-
egy for escaping from Prince Rabadash, he assumes they
will kill him if they discover who he is: "He had, you see,
no idea of how noble and free-born people behave" (p. 71).
But the model they provide him is a helpful one, as is that
of Prince Corin, for whom Shasta had been mistaken. The
"missing twin" motif, another well-established storyteller's
device, carries on the identity theme. Corin asks, when he
sees Shasta, "Who are you?" and Shasta replies, "I'm nobody, nobody in particular, I mean" (p. 74). But now he has
met a boy "almost exactly like himself" (p. 74), who provides him an example of openness and honesty:

> "You'll just have to tell them the truth, once I'm safely
> away."
> "What else did you think I'd be telling them?" asked the
> Prince with a rather angry look. (p. 76)

Shasta has time for reflection next day, as he waits among
the tombs: "He thought a good deal about the Narnians
and especially about Corin. He wondered what had happened when they discovered that the boy who had been
lying on the sofa and hearing all their secret plans wasn't
really Corin at all. It was very unpleasant to think of all
those nice people imagining him a traitor" (p. 88). Meeting
"nice people" and caring what they think about him is a
major step in the growth in his character.

The model Aravis finds, on the other hand, provides a
reminder of the kind of life she is fleeing from. As she
waits on a street for a litter to pass, she is recognized by
an old acquaintance, Lasaraleen Tarkheena, who takes her
and the horses home. Lasaraleen possesses the same

haughtiness and self-concern as Aravis, aggravated by self-indulgence and empty-headedness: "The fuss she made about choosing the dresses nearly drove Aravis mad. She remembered now that Lasaraleen had always been like that, interested in clothes and parties and gossip" (p. 96). Running through Aravis's adventure is a motif of disguise—she is disguised as her brother when she runs away from home, as a peasant when she enters Tashbaan, and as a slave-girl when she leaves. Disguise is another standard storyteller's device, one that is often used as a variant on the identity theme, symbolizing a confusion of identity for the person wearing the disguise. In this case it suggests that Aravis has not reached a comfortable level of self-acceptance—she seems to think the "common little boy" she is traveling with is "not good enough" for her (pp. 28, 31) and finds it painful to walk into Tashbaan as a peasant, rather than ride in "on a litter with soldiers before [her] and slaves behind" (p. 50). She comes to a clearer understanding of who she is and what she values by spending time with Lasaraleen and particularly by hearing Lasaraleen rebuke her for having a peasant boy as companion: "It's not Nice" (p. 99). Aravis "was so tired of Lasaraleen's silliness by now that, for the first time, she began to think that travelling with Shasta was really rather more fun than fashionable life in Tashbaan. So she only replied, 'You forget that I'll be a nobody, just like him, when we get to Narnia'" (p. 99). The answer is ironic, of course, for by now the reader has ample hints that Shasta will not be just a nobody in Narnia, but it signals the direction Aravis's growth will take, with a humility and acceptance new to her character.

The testing ground for the horses is the desert. From their adventures in Tashbaan, Shasta learned the best route across the desert and Aravis learned about the surprise attack on Archenland and Narnia planned by Prince Rabadash. As the horses and children set out to warn King

Lune of the danger, the grueling trip across the desert brings out the main attributes of the two horses. When the worst is over but the journey not yet complete, Bree insists on a rest and a snack, but Hwin replies, "I feel just like Bree that I *can't* go on. But when Horses have humans (with spurs and things) on their backs, aren't they often made to go on when they're feeling like this? and then they find they can. I m-mean—oughtn't we to be able to do even more, now that we're free" (p. 131). But she says it modestly and shyly and allows Bree to overwhelm her with his forceful assertion, "I think, Ma'am . . . that I know a little more about campaigns and forced marches and what a horse can stand than you do" (p. 131). Hwin is "a very sensible mare" (p. 45)—she, after all, thought up the plan they used for getting past Tashbaan. She must gain more confidence and assert herself a bit more, and slowly she does, for "it was really Hwin, though she was the weaker and more tired of the two, who set the pace" the rest of the way (p. 132).

It takes the threat of a lion, as they approach Archenland, to force Bree to begin to know himself. The contrast in the responses of Bree and Shasta to this danger reminds one again of the different directions their growth must take. Shasta's cry to Bree, as he sees the lion snapping at Hwin's heels and clawing at Aravis's back, "Must go back. Must help!" (p. 138), is a recognition of duty which overrides personal desire. He discovers the meaning of courage as he turns back to help Aravis and Hwin with no weapon and little chance of saving himself or them. All the awkwardness and self-consciousness are swallowed up as he responds to an as yet undefined desire to do the right thing, another indication of how he benefited from meeting the Narnians. As Shasta is ennobled, Bree faces the destruction of his self-conceit. In comparison with Shasta's bravery, Bree's desperate flight from the lion looks very much like cowardice. He says of it later, "[Shasta] ran in

90

the right direction: ran *back*. And that is what shames me most of all. I, who called myself a war horse and boasted of a hundred fights, to be beaten by a little human boy" (p. 145). In facing this shame Bree learns a first and necessary, but not yet adequate, lesson in humility.

The separation of Shasta and Bree is a further step in their progress toward identity and maturation. Shasta moves on into Narnia and initiation into adulthood (Chapters 12-13); Bree remains at the hermitage until, by giving up his illusions about his own worth, he becomes like a little child (Chapter 14). Shasta discovers that his act of courage was only the beginning of doing good and is sent running to King Lune, to learn "that if you do one good deed your reward usually is to be set to do another and harder and better one" (p. 140). After fulfilling his responsibility by warning the King about Rabadash's approach, he travels over the mountains and joins Corin and the Narnian army on its way to aid the Archenlanders. Now it is Shasta, rather than Bree, who participates in battle, not arrogantly but with determination: "It suddenly came into his head 'If you funk this, you'll funk every battle all your life. Now or never' " (p. 179). And though "he knows nothing about this work, . . . hasn't the faintest idea what to do with his sword" (p. 183), he again does what he believes he should and takes another major step toward adulthood. Bree needs rest rather than action, time to reflect upon the lessons he has been taught all his way. His host, the Hermit of the Southern March, becomes his mentor: "If you are really so humbled as you sounded a minute ago, you must learn to listen to sense. You're not quite the great horse you had come to think, from living among poor dumb horses. Of course you were braver and cleverer than *them*. You could hardly help being that. It doesn't follow that you'll be anyone very special in Narnia. But as long as you know you're nobody very special, you'll be a very decent sort of Horse" (p. 146). As Bree is discovering that

91

he is no longer a great Calormene war horse and that he must accept a new identity as an ordinary citizen of Narnia, Shasta is meeting King Lune and discovering his father and his identity—he is no longer Shasta, the common, self-conscious fisherman's child, but Cor, Crown Prince of Archenland.

Even before he learns his name, however, Shasta has found a deeper identity and his true Fatherland in a meeting with Aslan. Here again an idea in *Mere Christianity* is translated into an action of Narnia. Lewis discusses there what it is that "leads the Christian home" and summarizes it as "throw[ing] up the sponge," as recognizing one's personal inadequacy and putting "all his trust in Christ." The Christian begins to trust that "Christ will somehow share with him the perfect human obedience which He carried out from His birth to His crucifixion: that Christ will make the man more like Himself and, in a sense, make good his deficiencies. In Christian language, He will share His 'sonship' with us, will make us, like Himself, 'Sons of God' " (pp. 129, 128). To Lewis, "my true country" (p. 120) and full identity can be found only in a relationship outside the self, only in "handing everything over to Christ" (p. 129).

For all four main characters in *The Horse and His Boy* an encounter with Aslan is the final step in regaining their identity. Shasta meets Aslan on the road across the mountains into Narnia. As he rides along in the fog he notices the breathing of a creature beside him, but notices it "so gradually that he had really no idea how long it had been there" (p. 156). When he is told that the creature has been beside him all his life, comforting, protecting, and preparing for him, he asks, "Who *are* you?" " 'Myself,' said the Voice, very deep and low so that the earth shook: and again 'Myself,' loud and clear and gay: and then the third time 'Myself,' whispered so softly you could hardly hear it, and yet it seemed to come from all round you as if the leaves rustled with it" (p. 159). The reply alludes to the answer

God gave Moses when he asked the same question beside the burning bush, "I am" (Ex. 3:14), and it catches up in images the Christian idea of a God in three persons. Gradually the light increases and Shasta is able to see his companion: "After one glance at the Lion's face he slipped out of the saddle and fell at its feet. He couldn't say anything but then he didn't want to say anything, and he knew he needn't say anything" (p. 160). Having come to know Aslan, Shasta begins to love and to trust him.

Such trust relates directly to the important theme of Providence. Though present throughout the story, Providence stands out in an episode involving the Hermit of the Southern March. Aravis arrived at the Hermit's compound by escaping with only some scratches from the lion who chased her and Hwin. "I say," she exclaims, "I *have* had luck." The Hermit replies, "Daughter, . . . I have now lived a hundred and nine winters in this world and have never yet met any such thing as Luck" (p. 143). The word appears several other times in the book, each time in a situation where it emphasizes that none of the occurrences have been accidental (pp. 42, 158, and 162). From the apparently fortuitous encounter of Shasta and Bree at a remote cottage along the sea, to the seeming coincidence of a look-alike being seen and brought where he would learn directions across the desert, to the seemingly trivial recognition of Aravis by Lasaraleen, which put her in a position to learn of the plans to attack Archenland and Narnia, all was shaped and guided by Aslan. Talking to Shasta later, Aslan adds other details to fill out the plan: "I was the lion who forced you to join with Aravis. . . . I was the lion who gave the Horses the new strength of fear for the last mile so that you should reach King Lune in time. And I was the lion you do not remember who pushed the boat in which you lay, a child near death, so that it came to shore where a man sat, wakeful at midnight, to receive you" (p. 158). Aslan allowed Shasta to spend years in a disagreeable situation and then triggered a series of interrelated events in order to put Shasta in a position to "save Archenland from the deadliest danger in which ever she lay" (p. 198). In the words of Joseph, who underwent a similar series of unpleasant but important events, to the brothers who sold him into slavery, "Ye thought evil against me; but God meant it unto good, to bring to pass, as it is this day, to save much people alive" (Gen. 50:20).

The experiences of the other three characters are less dramatic, but in meeting Aslan they also confront their inadequacies and begin to trust in him. Bree, in his desire to be self-sufficient, asserts disdainfully that "it would be quite absurd to suppose he is a *real* lion" (p. 192), one which can *really* help or hurt those who need it. When a lion's whisker tickles his ear, he must face up to himself: "I'm afraid I must be rather a fool" (p. 193). His pretensions have been destroyed, his pride has been lost, and he enters his homeland "in a rather subdued frame of mind" (p. 200), aware "of how little he [knows] about Narnian customs and what dreadful mistakes he might make" (p. 201). He has become like a child, lacking experience and a settled sense of his identity, but now having a firm basis for regaining them. Aravis, when she meets Aslan, learns that she has encountered him before. It was Aslan who scratched her back to teach her an essential lesson: "The scratches on your back, tear for tear, throb for throb, blood for blood, were equal to the stripes laid on the back of your step-mother's slave because of the drugged sleep you cast upon her. You needed to know what it felt like" (p. 194). Aravis learns, on her journey, to know more about herself and to care more about others. "There's something I've got to say at once," she tells Shasta when he returns to the Hermit's compound. "I'm sorry I've been such a pig. But I did change before I knew you were a Prince, honestly I did" (p. 196). She has learned the humility and openness she needs for further growth and maturity. Hwin, from the leadership role pressed upon her on the journey, has gained assurance without losing her humility. When she sees the lion, though shaking with fear, she has the strength to trot directly across to him: " 'Please,' she said, 'you're so beautiful. You may eat me if you like. I'd sooner be eaten by you than fed by anyone else.' " In handing herself over to Aslan, she finds confirmation and affirmation of her being. "Dearest daughter, . . . I knew you would not be long in coming to me. Joy shall be yours" (p. 193). It is only after an encounter with Aslan, then, that they can truly be said, as they enter Archenland and the North, to be "returning to home and freedom" (p. 202).

The central theme of the loss and regaining of identity is summed up through Prince Rabadash in the final chapter. Like Shasta, now Prince Cor, Rabadash has met the Narnians in Tashbaan and been on a journey through the desert, but he has not profited from his experiences. In contrast to Cor's humility—"I do hope you won't think I'm got up like this (and the trumpeter and all) to try to impress you or make out that I'm different or any rot of that sort" (p. 196)—Rabadash is arrogant and defiant: "Learn who *I* am, horrible phantasm. I am descended from Tash, the inexorable, the irresistible" (p. 209). Of the major characters, only Rabadash claims to know Aslan already when he meets him: "I know you. You are the foul fiend of Narnia. You are the enemy of the gods" (p. 209). He obviously does not know Aslan, however, and he must learn that he does not know himself, does not realize that he is being an ass. He must learn the lessons of humility and submission that Cor and the others had to learn. "Forget your pride," Aslan urges him, "(what have you to be proud of?) and your anger (who has done you wrong?) and accept the mercy of these good kings" (p. 208). Because he will not give up the traits and actions which he thinks make him what he is, he must lose his identity. He can face up to what he is only by being turned physically into the ass he has already become through his attitude and behavior. He will regain his identity, "be healed" as Aslan puts it (p. 211), only by submitting himself to his own god, Tash. At the great Autumn Feast that year, he does stand before the altar of Tash and turn to "a man again" (p. 212) and eventually he becomes "the most peaceable Tisroc Calormen had ever known" (p. 212). But the change for Rabadash must come by the Calormene modes of compulsion and constraint, not in the joyful, fulfilling way by which Hwin, Bree, Aravis, and Shasta found themselves and freedom on their way to Narnia and Aslan.

7

"Putting the Human Machine Right": Moral Choice in *The Magician's Nephew*

L ITERATURE as a whole, according to archetypal critics, makes up a single story with a cyclical structure. This composite of all individual works of literature, or monomyth, is circular in shape and has four phases, which correspond to familiar cycles in human experience and to the most important narrative patterns. It might be diagrammed as follows:[1]

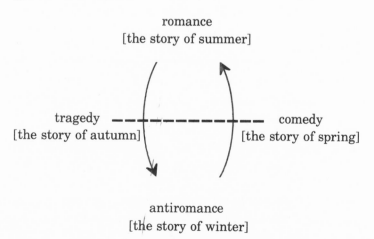

romance
[the story of summer]

tragedy   ——————————   comedy
[the story of autumn]   [the story of spring]

antiromance
[the story of winter]

97

The monomyth unifies literature as a whole, by establishing an outline into which individual stories and poems can be placed, and provides a structure which associates literature with human life, individually and totally.

The final two books of the Chronicles of Narnia relate closely to the structure of the monomyth. Lewis, surely, did not begin with these categories or this diagram in mind and design stories to fit them. But as he thought out accounts of the beginning and ending of Narnia and tried to see unity in the cycle of that world's history, Lewis, with his great knowledge of literature and archetypes, almost inevitably was led to use the pattern fundamental to nature and literature as the most appropriate for his purposes. Using in each story the dichotomies, or opposites, into which archetypes always fall, Lewis intertwines the accounts of two endings and two beginnings. Thus *The Magician's Nephew* moves from tragedy to comedy and reflects the archetypes of autumn and spring. And *The Last Battle* moves from antiromance to romance, through the archetypes of winter and summer. Approaching the two books through the four phases of the monomyth illuminates the artistry and themes of the stories, clarifies their deeper significance, stresses their unity, and indicates the importance of that unity.

The Magician's Nephew is best known for its account of the beginning of Narnia (a story of spring); but it begins with an account of the ending of another world (a story of autumn). The two children who are present at the creation of Narnia, Polly Plummer and Digory Kirke, go first to Charn and are present at its demise. *The Magician's Nephew* is a story of exploration. Polly and Digory go exploring first through an attic, which brings them unexpectedly into Uncle Andrew's study (Chapter 1), then, after a chapter of exposition, through the Wood between the Worlds, which brings them just as unexpectedly into the kingdom of Charn (Chapters 3-5) and later, again unexpectedly, into the world that becomes Narnia (Chapters 9-15). Such exploration in the plot prefigures a more significant kind, the exploration—central to the book's theme—of moral rules the characters must accept or reject and moral choices they must make.

It is in Charn that they encounter an autumn's tale of decline or a Fall. Northrop Frye characterizes the story of autumn as follows: "The sunset . . . phase. Myths of fall, . . . of violent death and sacrifice and of the isolation of the hero. . . . The archetype of tragedy and elegy" (*Fables of Identity,* p. 16). The images used in describing Charn echo these terms closely. The children are struck, as they arrive in Charn, by its age and silence:

> It was obviously very old. Many of the flat stones that paved the courtyard had cracks across them. None of them fitted closely together and the sharp corners were all worn off. One of the arched doorways was half filled up with rubble. . . . This place was at least as quiet as the quiet Wood between the Worlds. But it was a different kind of quietness. . . . This was a dead, cold, empty silence. (pp. 42-43)

Later, when the children see the sun over Charn, it gives a sense of sunset: "Low down and near the horizon hung a great, red sun, far bigger than our sun. Digory felt at once that it was also older than ours: a sun near the end of its life, weary of looking down upon that world" (pp. 58-59). Charn itself, "a vast city in which there was no living thing to be seen" (p. 59), was a victim of violence and cruelty. "I have stood here," Jadis the queen says, "(but that was near the end) when the roar of battle went up from every street and the river of Charn ran red" (p. 59). And the story is one of isolation—not, in this case, of the hero, but of the villainess: "Then I spoke the Deplorable Word. A moment later I was the only living thing beneath the sun" (p. 61).

The account of the last days of Charn is a tragic story,

not in its tone—for a children's story can never be fully tragic—but in its movement, the downward movement of the wheel of fortune from a high point to catastrophe. The account given by Jadis is of a nation which at one time was great and good, but which, in the ceaseless turning of fortune's wheel, fell as "all in one moment one woman blotted it out" (p. 60). The story, true to the nature of tragedy, carries a moral and confronts characters with moral choices. Moral rules, Lewis writes in the section of *Mere Christianity* on "Christian Behaviour," are "directions for running the human machine" and are concerned with three things: "Firstly, with fair play and harmony between individuals. Secondly, with what might be called tidying up or harmonising the things inside each individual. Thirdly, with the general purpose of human life as a whole: what man was made for" (pp. 69, 71). As the story describes the behavior of Uncle Andrew and Jadis, of Digory, and of Charn and Narnia, it is unified by its emphasis on the choices each must make between following and breaking those moral rules.

The issue of morality appears first in Uncle Andrew. Uncle Andrew is not interested in fair play or harmony with other individuals. The self-interest and vanity which led him to become a magician (p. 76) also lead to a total lack of concern for others. His immoral nature is communicated at a level children can understand readily by his cruelty to animals: "My earlier experiments were all failures. I tried them on guinea-pigs. Some of them only died. Some exploded like little bombs—" (p. 21). Young readers, many of whom, like Digory, have guinea pigs of their own, will understand. And they will see through the mean thing he does to Polly and Digory by tricking Polly into taking a yellow ring, which transports her into another world, and by forcing Digory to use a yellow ring in order to bring her the green ring she will need to return. When Uncle Andrew admits he had planned out the entire thing,

100

Digory reiterates the point for the readers: "You're simply a wicked, cruel magician like the ones in the stories" (p. 24).

Uncle Andrew is evil, but not unredeemably so. He is a dabbler in black magic, but one who lacks "the Mark" (pp. 55, 69) of those who have sold their souls to the art. Uncle Andrew's evil, in one sense, is only a pale reflection of the wickedness of Queen Jadis, to whom he is compared explicitly: both Uncle Andrew and Jadis, for example, break promises (pp. 18 and 60-61), believing that they are above conventional moral rules. And both end their claims to moral freedom with the words, "Ours . . . is a high and lonely destiny" (pp. 18 and 62), although, as Digory noticed, "they sounded much grander when Queen Jadis said them" (p. 62). Both have an "eager, almost a greedy" (p. 13) or "hungry and greedy" (p. 63) look on their faces, produced by their self-centeredness. As Uncle Andrew asserts his freedom to do as he pleased with his guinea pigs—"That's what the creatures were there for. I'd bought them myself" (p. 21), so Jadis claims that the common people of Charn were hers to do with as she pleased: "They were all *my* people. What else were they there for but to do my will" (p. 61). And both admit they have "paid a terrible price" (pp. 61, 20) to attain the evil knowledge and power they possess. Although Uncle Andrew may not be as wicked as Queen Jadis, the parallels between them point out the continuity in evil. The difference between slight evils and greater ones, between the "pantomime demon" (p. 11) and the supremely evil temptress, is a matter of degree, not of kind.

Despite the similarities between the temptation of Digory in the garden near the end of the story and the temptation in the biblical Garden of Eden, Jadis is not Satan. She is the White Witch of the first Chronicle and this book reveals more clearly than the first one her character as a Circe figure, the archetypal female temptress. In *The Lion, the Witch and the Wardrobe* Mr. Beaver traced her lineage to Lilith, the legendary first wife of Adam, who refused to be subordinate to Adam and to accept her roles as wife and mother. Jadis, in that tradition, opposes life and growth. She thrives in a world of cruelty and death, the kind of world she turned Charn into, but in the Wood between the Worlds, a womb-like area so full of latent life that "you could almost feel the trees growing" (p. 29), she loses her beauty and finds it hard to breathe, "as if the air of that place stifled her" (p. 67). Thus, later, she calls Narnia "a terrible world" (p. 102). Narnia too is full of life, a warm, creative world, very different from the cold, harsh worlds Jadis prefers: "This whole world was filled with a Magic different from hers and stronger. She hated it" (p. 101). Hers is the nature of a seductress, proud, cruel, destructive, oblivious to the need for fair play and harmony between herself and other individuals.

The second aspect of morality is illustrated by Digory, from whose perspective most of the story is told. Digory knows and accepts the traditional moral rules, as Uncle Andrew recognizes: "Oh, I see. You mean that little boys ought to keep their promises. Very true: most right and proper, I'm sure, and I'm very glad you have been taught to do it" (p. 18). He shows his courage and a sense of duty as he picks up a yellow ring and follows Polly on a journey into the unknown: "He could not *decently* have done anything else" (p. 27; italics added). But rules and decency are not sufficient when Digory sees the golden bell and the little golden hammer in Charn and reads the enchanted sign:

> Make your choice, adventurous Stranger;
> Strike the bell and bide the danger,
> Or wonder, till it drives you mad,
> What would have followed if you had. (p. 50)

He, like his uncle, is tempted with forbidden knowledge and gives in to the temptation.[2] Polly notices the similarity: "You looked exactly like your Uncle when you said that" (p. 50). He strikes the bell, which awakens the Witch, and he, with all Narnia, pays a terrible price. He claims later he was "enchanted by the writing under the bell" (p. 135), but Aslan corrects him: he was confronted with a moral decision and decided unwisely. There is need, then, for some tidying up or harmonizing inside Digory; his human machine needs to be put back in order, and the achievement of that is a significant thread running through the rest of the story.

The third moral area, concerning the general purpose of human life as a whole, is reflected in the total image of Charn. The rich and majestic Hall of Images which Digory and Polly discover in Charn, with magnificently clothed figures sitting on stone chairs along each side, depicts the changing character of the people of Charn.

> All the faces they could see [as they entered] were certainly nice. Both the men and women looked kind and wise, and they seemed to come of a handsome race. But after the children had gone a few steps down the room they came to faces that looked a little different. These were very solemn faces. You felt you would have to mind your P's and Q's, if you ever met living people who looked like that. When they had gone a little further, they found themselves among faces they didn't like: this was about the middle of the room. The faces here looked very strong and proud and happy, but they looked cruel. A little further on they looked crueller. Further on again, they were still cruel but they no longer looked happy. They were even despairing faces: as if the people they belonged to had done dreadful things and also suffered dreadful things. (pp. 47-48)

That the room represents the history of Charn is indicated by the empty chairs beyond the one Jadis was seated in: "There were plenty of empty chairs beyond her, as if the room had been intended for a much larger collection of images" (p. 48). Again the actions of a Narnian story—in this case the course of Charnian history—relate closely to the imagery of *Mere Christianity:*

> What Satan put into the heads of our remote ancestors was the idea that they could "be like gods"—could set up on their own as if they had created themselves—be their own masters—invent some sort of happiness for themselves outside God, apart from God. And out of that hopeless attempt has come nearly all that we call human history—money, poverty, ambition, war, prostitution, classes, empires, slavery—the long terrible story of man trying to find something other than God which will make him happy.
>
> The reason why it can never succeed is this. God made us: invented us as a man invents an engine. A car is made to run on gasoline, and it would not run properly on anything else. Now God designed the human machine to run on Himself. He Himself is the fuel our spirits were designed to burn, or the food our spirits were designed to feed on. There is no other. That is why it is just no good asking God to make us happy in our own way without bothering about religion. God cannot give us a happiness and peace apart from Himself, because it is not there. There is no such thing.
>
> That is the key to history. Terrific energy is expended—civilisations are built up—excellent institutions devised; but each time something goes wrong. Some fatal flaw always brings the selfish and cruel people to the top and it all slides back into misery and ruin. In fact, the machine conks. It seems to start up all right and runs a few yards, and then it breaks down. They are trying to run it on the wrong juice. (pp. 53-54)

Charn was intended to have a longer history, but Jadis in her pride and selfishness cut it short; and Charn was intended to have a happier history, but pride and selfishness, arising long before Jadis's time, distorted and spoiled it. The people of Charn at first were "kind and wise," as people were intended to be; but soon the selfish and cruel people came to the top and everything began to slide back into misery and ruin. Such is not the life people were made for: moral directions were needed to set the machine right.

The tragedy of Charn, however, does not complete the

story. The story of autumn, of decline or falling action, midway through the book, turns into a story of spring, a story of rising action, in which a happy ending grows out of circumstances which threaten to be catastrophic. After the children unintentionally take Jadis to London, occasioning the delightful account of her madcap adventures in that staid, sedate city, they manage to get her—along with Uncle Andrew, a cabby, and his horse—back to the Wood between the Worlds and from there they explore another world, the as yet "empty world" (p. 96) of Narnia. As they enter Narnia it is cold and dark, and the song the cabby begins singing about crops being safely gathered in is not entirely unsuitable after all (p. 97). Soon his autumn song is replaced by a song of spring, sung by a voice "deep enough to be the voice of the earth herself" (p. 98). It is the voice of Aslan, bringing into that world the light and warmth needed for life.

> Far away, and down near the horizon, the sky began to turn grey, ... grew slowly and steadily paler, ... [then] changed from white to pink and from pink to gold. The Voice rose and rose, till all the air was shaking with it. And just as it swelled to the mightiest and most glorious sound it had yet produced, the sun arose.
>
> Digory had never seen such a sun. The sun above the ruins of Charn had looked older than ours: this looked younger. You could imagine that it laughed for joy as it came up. ... The earth [it shone on] was of many colours: they were fresh, hot and vivid. (pp. 100-1)

Here indeed is the story of spring, of "dawn" and "birth" and "creation," as Frye characterizes it (*Fables of Identity*, p. 16). As the song continues, Narnia is clothed with grass and flowers, decorated with shrubs and trees, and populated with animals and insects. The creation reaches its climax when Aslan, having selected two of many kinds of animals to be talking animals, says, in the deepest wildest voice the children had ever heard, "Narnia, Narnia, Narnia, awake" (p. 116).

Lewis's creation account is one which children can respond to more easily than the biblical version, first, because they identify with the two children who are present at it and through whose eyes readers see what takes place, and, second, because of Lewis's use of detail: one can readily visualize the grass spreading out from the lion like a pool and running up the sides of little hills like a wave, or animals slowly, with some difficulty, emerging from the soil: "Can you imagine a stretch of grassy land bubbling like water in a pot? For that is really the best description of what was happening. In all directions it was swelling into humps. ... And the humps moved and swelled till they burst, and the crumbled earth poured out of them, and from each hump there came out an animal" (p. 113). Vivid as the details, drawn from several ancient creation stories,[3] are, they are less important than the total effect of the story. Parallel to the natural and deep-seated human need to know individual origins (the identity theme discussed in the last chapter) is the need, equally natural and deep-seated, to know the origin of the world. The desire is not so much to know the methods and details as to know the meaning and purpose behind it all. Lewis, therefore, is less concerned with the how than the who. The Son of God, who was the creator of our world (John 1:3; Hebrews 1:2), in his incarnation as Aslan is creator of Narnia. Aslan is the focal point of the scene, always present, always at the center of the important events at the moment. There is purposefulness, even an inexorability about his actions: "The Lion came on. Its walk was neither slower nor faster than before; you could not tell whether it even knew it had been hit" (p. 108). His impact on the scene and on the children is suggested by the narrator's comment about how exciting and vivid the colors of Narnia were, "until you saw the Singer himself, and then you forgot everything else" (p. 101). The character of the creator tells a great deal about the purpose of his creation: " 'Creatures,

I give you yourselves,' said the strong, happy voice of Aslan. 'I give to you forever this land of Narnia. I give you the woods, the fruits, the rivers. I give you the stars and I give you myself' " (p. 118). The purpose is to use and enjoy, to be their own persons and Aslan's.

Aslan's importance is brought home decisively when Polly concludes, with an unspeakable thrill, "that all the things were coming (as she said) 'out of the Lion's head' " (p. 107). Polly's words are very close to words Lewis used in talking about the Creation in *Mere Christianity:* "Christianity . . . thinks God made the world—that space and time, heat and cold, and all the colours and tastes, and all the animals and vegetables, are things that God 'made up out of his head' as a man makes up a story" (p. 45).[4] The passage goes on to state that Christianity "also thinks that a great many things have gone wrong with the world that God made and that God insists, and insists very loudly, on our putting them right again." Those passages, linking creation and moral choice so closely, clarify the structure and unity of *The Magician's Nephew.* The dominant quality of the book is the newness, vitality, and fecundity of the creation scene: that sense of life and growth lingers on as the principal flavor of the story. But one can never disassociate it completely from the sense of defeat and death that preceded it, in the story of Charn. And Lewis's point is that the two never can be separated. Life leads, inevitably, to choice and choice, just as inevitably, to wrong decisions. There is a tinge of death, then, mixed in with the dominant theme of "life" in *The Magician's Nephew,* and Lewis's combining of the archetypal stories of autumn and spring captures that mixture nicely. At its birth corruption entered Narnia: "Before the new, clean world I gave you is seven hours old, a force of evil has already entered it" (p. 136). Even in spring, in the newness and freshness of birth and growth, the seeds of autumn are planted. The tragic seed cannot be rooted out; in the cycle of things, it will bear fruit; but the cycle does allow time for a comic season before the inevitable harvest: "Evil will come of that evil, but it is still a long way off, and I will see to it that the worst falls upon myself. In the meantime, let us take such order that for many hundred years yet this shall be a merry land in a merry world" (p. 136). The language reflects the archetype: this is the essence of comedy, as a potential catastrophe is averted (in this case temporarily) and a happy ending results. Digory, who brought the evil from the wasteland of Charn, is sent to a garden—the contrasting images are important—for the means to contain that evil.

The journey to the garden for the silver apple which can protect Narnia completes the morality themes introduced in the first half of the book. Digory's journey is the archetypal journey of testing and growth. He first is tempted to take an apple for himself: "Could it be wrong to taste one?" (p. 158). He resists the temptation in part through his early moral training and in part through the glance of a Phoenix who was roosting in the tree above him. The Phoenix is traditionally a symbol of resurrection and here it seems (like the albatross in *The Voyage of the "Dawn Treader"*) to be an embodiment of Aslan. Digory then is tempted with the kind of power Uncle Andrew and Jadis craved early in the story: "Eat it, Boy, eat it; and you and I will both live forever and be king and queen of this whole world" (p. 161). This temptation Digory shrugs off easily, for he has no desire for power and glory. Finally, he is tempted to substitute his own, personal desire—bringing health to his mother, who has been near death throughout the story—for the broader purpose Aslan had in mind, of making Narnia "the kindly land I mean it to be" (p. 175). The Witch urges him, "Use your Magic and go back to your own world. A minute later you can be at your Mother's bedside, giving her the fruit. . . . Soon she will be quite well again. All will be well again" (pp. 161-62). This temptation, with its mixture of unselfishness, is the great test. The language used in describing Digory's dilemma reminds one of the "terrible price" Uncle Andrew and Jadis paid to gain their ends: "He now knew that the most terrible choice lay before him" (p. 162). He is able to resist the temptation, however, when Jadis suggests to him the kind of measures she and Uncle Andrew had used, the breaking of his promise to Aslan (p. 162) and the nasty trick of leaving Polly behind: "The meanness of the suggestion . . . suddenly made all the other things the Witch had been saying to him sound false and hollow" (p. 163). Through his adventure, Digory has grown in strength and spirit: he has achieved an inner harmony that allows him to face and resist the most powerful of temptations to evil.

Lewis uses the episode in the garden to make an important point about the theme of morality, the traditional point that one's choices determine what one is. Early in the book Digory challenges Uncle Andrew, "You're simply a wicked, cruel magician like the ones in the stories. Well, I've never read a story in which people of that sort weren't paid out in the end, and I bet you will be. And serve you right" (p. 24). The stories Digory had read may well have been reflecting an old moral principle which Lewis sums up in *Mere Christianity:*

> People often think of Christian morality as a kind of bargain in which God says, "If you keep a lot of rules I'll reward you, and if you don't I'll do the other thing." I do not think that is the best way of looking at it. I would much rather say that every time you make a choice you are turning the central part of you, the part of you that chooses, into something a little different from what it was before. And taking your life as a whole, with all your innumerable choices, all your life long you are slowly turning this central thing either into a heavenly creature or into a hellish creature. (p. 86)

This is reaffirmed in the lines written on the gates of the garden near the end of the book: "For those who steal or those who climb my wall / Shall find their heart's desire and find despair" (p. 157). Jadis, who has always sought power and been willing to pay any price for it, climbs the wall, steals an apple, and finds both her desire and despair: "She has won her heart's desire; she has unwearying strength and endless days like a goddess. But length of days with an evil heart is only length of misery and already she begins to know it. All get what they want: they do not always like it" (p. 174). The last sentence applies equally well to Uncle Andrew. He got the magical powers he wanted, but in doing so he cut himself off from nature as well as from other human beings. Aslan's line, as he gives Uncle Andrew the only comfort he can, echoes the line on the garden gate: "Sleep and be separated for some few hours from all the torments you have desired for yourself" (p. 171). On the other hand, Digory's choices, after the unfortunate one in the Hall of Images in Charn, steadily strengthen his character and earn him, upon his return to Aslan with the apple, the accolade "Well done" (p. 166). He is a good and faithful servant, preparing himself to enter into the joys of his Lord.

The importance of choice also enters the moral area which was introduced by the story of Charn in the first half of the book and which is extended through the story of Narnia to our world. Charn, though its actual life had ended long before through violence and cruelty, reached the time of its dissolution late in the book: "That world is ended, as if it had never been" (p. 178). Narnia had, and continues to have, the potential to become "another strong and cruel empire like Charn" (p. 175) if its people themselves become cruel and selfish. But that danger is even greater for our world, and Aslan cites Charn as a lesson to us:

> "Let the race of Adam and Eve take warning."
> "Yes, Aslan," said both the children. But Polly added, "But we're not quite as bad as that world, are we, Aslan?"

"Not yet, Daughter of Eve," he said. "Not yet. But you are growing more like it. It is not certain that some wicked one of your race will not find out a secret as evil as the Deplorable Word and use it to destroy all living things. And soon, very soon, before you are an old man and an old woman, great nations in your world will be ruled by tyrants who care no more for joy and justice and mercy than the Empress Jadis. Let your world beware." (p. 178)

Surely those who see a contemporary social comment in the passage are correct. According to the "Outline of Narnian history so far as it is known,"[5] Digory and Polly were born in 1888 and 1889, respectively, and were carried into Narnia by the rings in 1900. Well before they were old, their world had seen a Hitler and a Stalin and had learned to live with the fear of an evil secret, the atomic bomb. But the impact of the passage goes deeper as well: the fate of our world, too, will be determined by its choices. The people of our world must decide if, by becoming selfish and cruel, they will draw tyranny upon themselves, or if they will resist the temptations of power and possessions and will live instead in the joy and justice, mercy and peace that were intended for them.

The contrasting possibilities of oppression and joy are reflected in the book's images of country and city, which traditionally have been used to symbolize good and evil, the idyllic and the undesirable, respectively. Although Charn is, of course, the prime example of evil associated with a city, it is not the only one. There is also the oppressiveness of London, noted first in the opening chapter: Digory tells Polly she would cry too, "if you'd lived all your life in the country and had a pony, and a river at the bottom of the garden, and then been brought to live in a beastly Hole like this" (p. 3). Later, the horse Strawberry complains about London: "It was a hard, cruel country. . . . There was no grass. All hard stones." And the cabbie's reply makes the city-country contrast come out explicitly:

"Too true, mate, too true. . . . A 'ard world it was. I always did say those paving-stones weren't fair on any 'oss. That's Lunn'on, that is. I didn't like it no more than what you did. You were a country 'oss, and I was a country man. Used to sing in the choir, I did, down at 'ome. But there wasn't a living for me there" (p. 123). Narnia, on the other hand, is the emblem of country, where a king is expected to be able to "use a spade and a plough and raise food out of the earth" (p. 139), and its goodness is manifest in the effect it has on those who have been corrupted by the city, especially the cabby—his voice becomes "more like the country voice he must have had as a boy and less like the sharp, quick voice of a cockney" (p. 139), and his behavior too becomes more gentle: "All the sharpness and cunning and quarrelsomeness which he had picked up as a London cabby seemed to have been washed away, and the courage and kindness which he had always had were easier to see" (p. 167). It is almost inevitable, then, that the story should end with Digory and his family moving to a "great big house in the country" where things will "go on getting better and better" for them all (p. 183).

The tragic story of Charn has turned, at least for now, into the comic story of Narnia, and the book ends with a symbolically happy ending. Digory's mother, who has been seriously ill from the beginning of the story, is restored to health—it was "like a miracle" (p. 182); his father receives a large inheritance and can retire and come home from India for ever and ever; Polly comes to visit Digory in the country nearly every holiday and learns "to ride and swim and milk and bake and climb" (p. 184). In Narnia "the Beasts lived in great peace and joy and neither the Witch nor any other enemy came to trouble that pleasant land for many hundred years" (p. 184). It is indeed an ending that could lead one to think "they were all going to live happily ever after" (pp. 183-84). But the happy ending is not assured yet, for this is only the beginning of the story of Narnia. Much hardship, sorrow, and pain must occur before the truly happy ending is reached, some twenty-five-hundred years later, at the conclusion of *The Last Battle.*[6]

8

"My True Country":
Longing in *The Last Battle*

*I*F *The Magician's Nephew* responds to the human hunger to know of the beginning of things, *The Last Battle* fulfills the need for knowledge about the end. Northrop Frye describes the last of his four phases as the "darkness, winter and dissolution phase. Myths of the triumphs of these powers; myths of floods and the return of chaos, of the defeat of the hero" (*Fables of Identity,* p. 16). This describes well the pattern Lewis found best suited to his account of the dissolution and destruction of the Narnian society and world. But for Lewis, as a Christian, dissolution is not the end and *The Last Battle* concludes in the second phase, "the zenith, summer, and . . . triumph phase. Myths . . . of entering into Paradise" (*Fables of Identity,* p. 16). *The Last Battle* moves, then, from the mode of irony, or "antiromance," the essence of human anxiety dreams, to romance, which pictures idealized human experience and complete happiness. Out of a tone of fear, it creates and builds a tone of longing, which, though strongest at the end of the book, is present throughout and becomes the unifying quality of the story.

The sense of frustration that dominates the first half of *The Last Battle* grows out of the first striking image in the book. When Puzzle the Donkey is induced by Shift the Ape to plunge into Caldron Pool and retrieve the yellow thing that just came over the waterfall, the description of Puzzle's struggle becomes a symbol of the story that is to follow:

> A great mass of foam got him in the face and filled his mouth with water and blinded him. Then he went under altogether for a few seconds, and when he came up again he was in quite another part of the Pool. Then the swirl caught him and carried him round and round and faster and faster till it took him right under the waterfall itself, and the force of the water plunged him down, deep down, so that he thought he would never be able to hold his breath till he came up again. (pp. 4-5)

The land of Narnia, as Shift proceeds to betray it to Calormen and to undercut its belief in Aslan and in itself, is similarly caught in a maelstrom. It struggles—behind the hasty and misguided efforts of King Tirian and Jewel the Unicorn, then with the help of the children Jill and Eustace, and finally through arguing against error and fighting it in battle—to get free of the current that is pulling it down. Again and again a feeling of optimism carries Narnia to the surface, but it is plunged down each time and eventually, at the end of the battle, it, unlike Puzzle, is submerged for good.

The setting in the early part of the story creates a foreboding, even despairing tone, and, by contrast, a deep sense of longing for Narnia. Tirian is first encountered, for example, at a little hunting lodge "where he often stayed for ten days or so in the pleasant spring weather" (p. 12). It is there that he hears the "wonderful news" that Aslan has come to Narnia again (p. 13). As Jill and Eustace walk with Tirian, after being brought to Narnia in answer to his cry for help and freeing him from the Calormenes, "the sun had risen, dewdrops were twinkling on every branch, and birds were singing" (p. 47). Later, when the King with his now larger group of followers sets out toward Cair Par-

avel to organize the army and attack the invaders in a
unified way, it was "the first really warm day of that spring.
The young leaves seemed to be much further out than yesterday: the snowdrops were over, but they saw several
primroses. The sunlight slanted through the trees, birds
sang, and always (though usually out of sight) there was
the noise of running water" (p. 87). Such details, on the
one hand, intensify the love of and desire for Narnia: "The
children felt, 'This is really Narnia at last'" (p. 87) and
Jill thinks, "Wouldn't it be lovely if Narnia just went on
and on—like what you said it has been?" (p. 89). And, on
the other hand, they instill a false sense of optimism, even
in Tirian, whose "heart grew lighter as he walked ahead
of them, humming an old Narnian marching song" (p. 87).

But constantly there are reminders that the optimism
is false hope and that Narnia will not go on and on. The
opening words of the book are "in the last days of Narnia"
(p. 1) and the first reference to Tirian describes him as "the
last of the Kings of Narnia" (p. 12). The foreboding tone
continues when Roonwit the Centaur reports that he finds,
as he studies the stars, "terrible things written in the skies"
(p. 15). Shortly thereafter, when Tirian and Jewel go alone
and in haste to stop the murder of the trees, Tirian feels
"horrible thoughts aris[ing] in my heart" and the narrator
comments that "much evil came of their rashness" (p. 20).
And as the children and Tirian walk through the woods on
their way to Stable Hill, the silence all around them conveys the mood of the whole country: "Gloom and fear
reigned over Narnia" (p. 59). Nowhere is the effect of the
contrasting tones, of optimism and fear, of hope and doom,
more striking than at the end of the scene of beauty and
lifted spirits described above. Immediately after Tirian felt
his heart grow lighter and Jill expressed her hope that
Narnia would go on and on, Jewel cautions that "all worlds
draw to an end; except Aslan's own country" (p. 89) and
Farsight the eagle arrives to report that Cair Paravel has

[margin note: Reminds me of Ruth; God not mentioned but is found throughout]

been captured and Roonwit their messenger has been killed. There will be no help and there is no more reason for hope: as the King says after a long silence, "Narnia is no more" (p. 91). The springtime setting and the beauty of the countryside have increased the children's desires for Narnia, in order to intensify by contrast their growing despair at its approaching defeat.

A fourth-phase narrative, a story of defeat and dissolution, according to Frye, employs the mode of irony, or antiromance. It is striking, therefore, that *The Last Battle* is the only one of the Chronicles to use irony. From its opening scene, it requires that a reader discern the discrepancy between reality and appearance. As Shift explains why Puzzle, rather than Shift, should plunge into the pool for the lion skin, the expressed reasons are definitely not the real ones: " 'Wanting *me* to go into the water,' said the Ape. 'As if you didn't know perfectly well what weak chests Apes always have and how easily they catch cold! Very well. I *will* go in. I'm feeling cold enough already in this cruel wind. But I'll go in. I shall probably die. Then you'll be sorry' " (p. 4). That tone appears again and again early in the book, as for example when Shift asks Puzzle to try on the coat he has fashioned out of the lion skin while Puzzle was trudging to Chippingford for oranges and bananas: " 'You *are* unkind, Puzzle,' said Shift. 'If *you're* tired, what do you think *I* am? All day long, while you've been having a lovely refreshing walk down the valley, I've been working hard to make you a coat. My paws are so tired I can hardly hold these scissors. And now you won't say thank-you—and you won't even look at the coat—and you don't care—and—and—' " (pp. 8-9). Establishment of such discrepancies, between what words or actions seem to be and what they really are, is verbal irony. It is not very sophisticated irony—a child has no trouble seeing through the deception. But that is just the point, for the irony becomes a key indicator that the Ape and his side are not to be trusted.

Such verbal ironies reappear in the fourth chapter as the Ape informs the Narnians about conditions under the new regime, and they grow into a vein of satire on political and religious tendencies in Lewis's day. The Ape, in the passage touching on politics, tells the other animals to get ideas of freedom out of their heads. "Everybody who can work is going to be made to work in the future. Aslan has it all settled with the King of Calormen. . . . All you horses and bulls and donkeys are to be sent down into Calormen to work for your living—pulling and carrying the way horses and such do in other countries. And all you digging animals like moles and rabbits and Dwarfs are going down to work in the Tisroc's mines" (p. 29). But this, he assures them, will not be slavery: "You'll be paid—very good wages too. That is to say, your pay will be paid into Aslan's treasury and he will use it all for everybody's good. . . . It's all arranged. And all for your own good. We'll be able, with the money you earn, to make Narnia a country worth living in. There'll be oranges and bananas pouring in—and roads and big cities and schools and offices and whips and muzzles and saddles and cages and kennels and prisons— Oh, everything" (p. 30). The lines almost surely reflect Lewis's concern over the increasing tendency, in our day, toward collectivism and oligarchy. He wrote in 1958, "The modern State exists not to protect our rights but to do us good or make us good—anyway, to do something to us or make us something. Hence the new name 'leaders' for those who were once 'rulers.' We are less their subjects than their wards, pupils, or domestic animals. There is nothing left of which we can say to them, 'Mind your own business.' Our whole lives *are* their business."[1] This tendency has come at the same time as a loss of personal freedom: "Two wars necessitated vast curtailments of liberty, and we have grown, though grumblingly, accustomed to our chains. The increasing complexity and precariousness of our economic life have forced Government to take over many spheres of activity once left to choice or chance."[2] To point toward the dangers in that trend Lewis has the Ape say, in reply to the Bear's assertion that "we want to be free," "What do you know about freedom? You think freedom means doing what you like. Well, you're wrong. That isn't true freedom. True freedom means doing what I tell you" (pp. 30-31).

The religious equivalent to this political tyranny is the Ape's insidious attack on belief in Aslan. It begins with the argument that everyone actually believes in the same thing: "Tash is only another name for Aslan. All that old idea of us being right and the Calormenes wrong is silly. We know better now. The Calormenes use different words but we all mean the same thing. Tash and Aslan are only two different names for you know Who" (p. 31). In forming that argument, the Ape twists Puzzle's reverent, awe-filled reference to "you know Who" (p. 6) into an irreverent, meaningless generality. This sort of thing becomes the Narnian version of the liberal accommodation and whittling down of the truth of the Gospel that Lewis complained about in our world: "I have some definite views about the de-Christianizing of the church," he commented in an interview in 1963. "I believe that there are many accommodating preachers, and too many practitioners in the church who are not believers. Jesus Christ did not say 'Go into all the world and tell the world that it is quite right.' The Gospel is something completely different. In fact, it is directly opposed to the world."[3] From accommodation of liberal ideas it is an easy step, or slip, to rejection of the fundamental ideas of the faith: Lewis often heard, from churchmen in his day, doctrine which was "so 'broad' or 'liberal' or 'modern' that it in fact excludes any real Supernaturalism and thus ceases to be Christian at all."[4] The Narnian world experienced a somewhat similar situation, as a conversation between Ginger the Cat and

Rishda Tarkhaan, the Calormene commander, illustrates: " 'I just wanted to know exactly what we both meant today about Aslan meaning *no more* than Tash.' 'Doubtless, most sagacious of cats,' says the other, 'you have perceived my meaning.' 'You mean,' says Ginger, 'that there's no such person as either.' 'All who are enlightened know that,' said the Tarkaan" (p. 79).

The attack on Narnia by her enemies is so effective, so devastating, because it undermines the principles and values on which Narnia was founded. Aslan intended Narnia to be free and he reminded King Frank that the animals he would rule over "are not slaves like the dumb beasts of the world you were born in but Talking Beasts and free subjects" (*The Magician's Nephew,* p. 139). And at the creation of Narnia Aslan said to the animals, "I give you myself" (*The Magician's Nephew,* p. 118). He is not a tame lion, but when Digory asked Aslan to cure his mother, "great shining tears stood in the Lion's eyes . . . [and Digory] felt as if the Lion must really be sorrier about his Mother than he was himself" (*The Magician's Nephew,* p. 142). Narnia was intended, then, to be a "kindly land" (*The Magician's Nephew,* p. 175), a land of obedience, love, and freedom. To see these values undermined is almost as hard as to see the nation itself fall. And the use of the ironic mode to depict the undermining is effective because irony and satire remind the reader of normal, positive values as they poke fun at and criticize departures from those values.

Despite the coming of the children in response to Tirian's prayer-like call, "Aslan! Aslan! Aslan! Come and help us Now" (p. 41), the situation in Narnia continues to decline. Narnia continues to be endangered by those from without who "care neither for Tash nor Aslan but have only an eye to their own profit" (p. 79) and by those from within who begin accepting the same premise: "We're on our own now. . . . The Dwarfs are for the Dwarfs" (p. 73).

The extent of the Ape's commitment to those values becomes clear only after the faithful few learn of the attack
on Cair Paravel: "We see that the Ape's plans were laid
deeper than we dreamed," Jewel comments. "Doubtless he
has been long in secret traffic with the Tisroc, and as soon
as he had found the lionskin, he sent him word to make
ready his navy for the taking of Cair Paravel and all Narnia. Nothing now remains for us seven but to go back to
Stable Hill, proclaim the truth, and take the adventure
that Aslan sends us." Brave as Jewel's words are, the situation as a whole appears hopeless: "If, by a great marvel,
we defeat those thirty Calormenes who are with the Ape,
[we must] turn again and die in battle with the far greater
host of them that will soon march from Cair Paravel"
(pp. 92-93).

The despairing tone in *The Last Battle* is supported by
imagery of darkness, death, and dissolution, all characteristic of the ironic mode. Shift figures, for example, that
someone who saw Puzzle in his lion skin "just might mis-
take him for a lion, if he didn't come too close, and if the
light was not too good" (p. 9). The false Aslan, partly for
that reason, is shown only at night, at "dreadful midnight
meetings" (p. 78), and consultations between the enemy
generally are held at times and places that are "black as
pitch" (p. 78). In keeping with the long tradition of romances the evil characters are dark, "our dark-faced friends,
the Calormenes," as the Ape calls them (p. 29). When the
evil god Tash passes through Narnia, it is as if a previously
sunny day was "clouding over" (p. 79). The last battle is
fought at night, with firelight outlining objects, and the
inside of the stable, especially to the dwarfs, is "pitch-black"
(p. 144). All of the darkness and blackness creates an
atmosphere of doubt and dread and reinforces the despair
which was already growing out of early events.

Death is first mentioned in *The Last Battle* as the seven
loyal Narnians are on their way toward Stable Hill and

Eustace wonders, "What'll happen if we get killed here?" Will they still be alive in England, or will they vanish and never be heard of any more? Jill begins to reply, stops, then begins again:

> "I *was* going to say I wished we'd never come. But I don't, I don't, I don't. Even if we *are* killed. I'd rather be killed fighting for Narnia than grow old and stupid at home and perhaps go about in a bathchair and then die in the end just the same."
>
> "Or be smashed up by British Railways!"
>
> "Why d'you say that?"
>
> "Well when that awful jerk came—the one that seemed to throw us into Narnia—I thought it *was* the beginning of a railway accident. So I was jolly glad to find ourselves here instead." (pp. 96-97)

Later the children discover that there was indeed a railway accident, in which the other friends of Narnia and the Pevensie children's parents were killed. Lewis resolves the dilemma about the effect of death in one world on the other world by setting up a death situation in both: Jill and Eustace are drawn into Narnia in the split second before their deaths in our world and that, because of the different time sequences, makes it possible for them to die simultaneously in both worlds.

There have been deaths, of course, in the earlier Chronicles: they are inevitable in the romance tradition, with its adventures and battles, and can be viewed as something children should be introduced to as a natural part of life. At the conclusion of *The Silver Chair* Lewis made a special effort to take the fearfulness out of death by depicting it as a transition to a new and more glorious existence. But death in the earlier books has involved characters with whom the readers are not closely identified, at least not at the time of their deaths. In *The Last Battle,* however, the characters facing imminent death are Jill and Eustace, with whom readers have identified in earlier books as well as this one, and Tirian, the character from whose viewpoint most of this story is being related. To bring death so close without imposing an impossible emotional burden on young readers required most careful handling. Lewis solved the problem by use of the stable door.

The stable door becomes, throughout the battle, a symbol of death. Lewis can achieve the authenticity of having his characters die in a losing battle, without the naturalistic detail unnecessary in a fairy tale, by having his characters pass through the stable door into eternity. The Calormene leader, Rishda Tarkaan, orders that the Narnians be offered as a sacrifice to Tash: "Take all of them alive if you can and hurl them into the Stable: or drive them into it. When they are all in we will put fire to it and make them an offering to the great god Tash" (p. 117). Though the offerings are to be live offerings, the symbolism of death is clear. As Poggin the Dwarf looks at the stable, he remarks, "I feel in my bones . . . that we shall all, one by one, pass through that dark door before morning" and Tirian replies, "It is indeed a grim door" (p. 128). When the children have passed through it they meet the others who died in the train crash: Professor Kirke, Aunt Polly, Peter, Edmund, and Lucy. Death and the door are, in effect and meaning, the same. The important thing is that neither represents an end but a beginning, not an exit but an entrance.

After death comes the final stage of a fourth-phase narrative, dissolution. After the battle, Aslan appears and summons Father Time, who, as it was foretold in an earlier story, "would wake on the day the world ended" and henceforth have a new name, Eternity (p. 150). Aslan then summons the creatures of the Narnian world—those who have been dead, like Roonwit the Centaur, Jewel the Unicorn, the boar, the bear, and the horses (p. 154), and those who have not died: some were living in distant parts of Narnia or in foreign countries, while others were at Stable Hill but "just crept quietly away during the fighting" (p. 120). The door now symbolizes the entrance to paradise, the way of acceptance. Aslan stands at the doorway, on its left side, as the creatures approach him:

> As they came right up to Aslan one or other of two things happened to each of them. They all looked straight in his face; I don't think they had any choice about that. And when some looked, the expression of their faces changed terribly—it was fear and hatred: except that, on the faces of Talking Beasts, the fear and hatred lasted only for a fraction of a second. You could see that they suddenly ceased to be *Talking* Beasts. They were just ordinary animals. And all the creatures who looked at Aslan in that way swerved to their right, his left, and disappeared into his huge black shadow, which . . . streamed away to the left of the doorway. The children never saw them again. I don't know what became of them. But the others looked in the face of Aslan and loved him, though some of them were very frightened at the same time. And all these came in at the Door, in on Aslan's right. (pp. 153-54)[5]

Aslan had already called the stars home, leaving "spreading blackness, . . . emptiness" behind (p. 151). The image of darkness is reinforced by images of water and then ice. After dragons and lizards reduce Narnia to a desert, "a foaming wall of water" comes across it: "The sea was rising. . . . All now was level water from where they stood to where the water met the sky" (pp. 155-56). The dying sun then licked up the moon and was squeezed to death by Father Time, "and instantly there was total darkness" (p. 157). Finally comes the cold: "Everyone except Aslan jumped back from the ice-cold air which now blew through the Doorway. Its edges were already covered with icicles" (p. 157). *The Last Battle,* then, goes beyond an account of the decline of a nation or world (a story of autumn) to its dissolution, to a story of winter, the central image of Frye's fourth phase.[6] Lewis's choice of ending was probably influenced by the Icelandic myths he loved greatly throughout his life. But the question of a specific source is not important: it was the "right" conclusion archetypally, the one needed to convey with fullest impact the end of things, the completion of the cycle of nature and of the history of Narnia.[7]

The larger part of *The Last Battle* is a winter's tale, an account of the final days of Narnian history presented through images of darkness, death, and dissolution. But the end of Narnian history is not the end of the story. As Tirian is thrown through the stable door, the imagery shifts abruptly: "It was not dark inside the Stable, as he had expected. He was in strong light" (p. 131). Indeed, he and Jill and Eustace and Peter, Edmund, Lucy, Aunt Polly, and the Professor, in whose company he finds himself, are not in the stable at all: "They stood on grass, the deep blue sky was overhead, and the air which blew gently on their faces was that of a day in early summer" (p. 136). The story of winter, of dissolution, has given way to a story of summer, of triumph, of entry into paradise, and of the ideal, wish-fulfillment dream of romance.

The sense of longing which was created intermittently in the earlier part of the story now intensifies greatly. The place Tirian has entered is a country of youth: as Jill puts it, the Professor and Aunt Polly aren't "much older than we are here" (p. 139). It is a place of health—Edmund's knee ceases to be sore and the Professor suddenly feels unstiffened; and abundance—they have crowns on their heads and are in glittering clothes; and freedom—"I've a feeling we've got to the country where everything is allowed" (p. 137). And it is a place of beauty and of bounty: "Not far away from them rose a grove of trees, thickly leaved, but under every leaf there peeped out the gold or faint yellow or purple or glowing red of fruits such as no one has seen in our world," fruits compared with which "the freshest grapefruit you've ever eaten was dull, and the juiciest orange was dry, and the most melting pear was hard and woody, and the sweetest wild strawberry was sour." After doing his best to say what it was like, the narrator confesses his inadequacy: "But I can't describe it. You can't find out what it is like unless you can get to that country and taste for yourself" (pp. 136-37).

Most of all, it is the place where those who love and long for Aslan find fulfillment. Soon after entering Narnia, Tirian sees a brightness and turns around: "There stood his heart's desire, huge and real, the golden Lion, Aslan himself" (p. 146). Here is the real object of all the unsatisfied and unsatisfiable longings experienced on earth: "If I find in myself a desire which no experience in this world can satisfy, the most probable explanation is that I was made for another world. . . . I must [therefore] keep alive in myself the desire for my true country, which I shall not find till after death" (*Mere Christianity,* p. 120). Jewel's words echo those sentiments closely: "I have come home at last! This is my real country! I belong here. This is the land I have been looking for all my life, though I never knew it till now" (p. 171). It is also the land that Emeth, the Calormene officer, has been looking for all his life, though he didn't know it until now. Because of his great desire for God and goodness, for wisdom and understanding, which he thought were embodied in Tash, harsh and cruel though he might seem to others, he is admitted to the New Narnia. In desiring and doing good, he was actually serving Aslan, not Tash, and the God of truth and love accepts his service as unto himself.[8] Emeth believes, and he can see: "As soon as I had gone through the door, the first wonder was that I found myself in this great sunlight" (p. 163). The Dwarfs, on the other hand, do not believe and cannot see. They find only a small dark stable on the other side of the door. "How in the name of all Humbug can I see what ain't there? And how can I see you any more than you can see me in this pitch darkness?" (p. 144). Even Aslan can do little for them: the rich feast he provides tastes to them like stable litter. "They will not let us help them. They have chosen cunning instead of belief. Their prison is only in their own minds, yet they are in that prison" (p. 148). And presumably they are in it still. Dante, in *The Divine Comedy,* left those who were unwilling to commit themselves to goodness or evil outside heaven and hell—neither place would accept them. Perhaps it is similar in the Narnian situation. The Dwarfs, after all, are for the Dwarfs: they fire arrows at talking horses and at Calormenes. Thus they neither disappear into Aslan's shadow nor enter the new Narnia. Because Aslan was not their heart's desire, because they did not long for his country, they apparently remain forever in that "pitch-black, poky, smelly little hole of a stable" (p. 144).

The others, who have longed for Narnia as well as for Aslan, discover that they have both. Farsight the Eagle sums it up for the others: "We have all been blind. We are only beginning to see where we are. From up there I have seen it all—Ettinsmuir, Beaversdam, the Great River, and Cair Paravel still shining on the edge of the Eastern Sea. Narnia is not dead. This is Narnia" (p. 169). As he has tried to convey ideas about Christianity through the images of Narnia, so Lewis now tries to put Plato's theory of ideas into images. First the Professor explains that the Narnia to which the Pevensie children could not return was not the real Narnia: "That had a beginning and an end. It was only a shadow or a copy of the real Narnia, which has always been here and always will be here. . . . And of course it is different; as different as a real thing is from a shadow or as waking life is from a dream" (pp. 169-70). Such idealistic philosophy is, of course, difficult to get across successfully, and Lewis tries to clarify it by an analogy:

Perhaps you will get some idea of it, if you think like this.

You may have been in a room in which there was a window that looked out on a lovely bay of the sea or a green valley that wound away among mountains. And in the wall of that room opposite to the window there may have been a looking glass. And as you turned away from the window you suddenly caught sight of that sea or that valley, all over again, in the looking glass. And the sea in the mirror, or the valley in the mirror, were in one sense just the same as the real ones: yet at the same time they were somehow different—deeper, more wonderful, more like places in a story: in a story you have never heard but very much want to know. (p. 170)

Lewis's comparison captures, by the distancing effect of a mirror's reflection, a sense of wonder and inaccessibility and it reinforces his point that the "reality" of the physical world out the window is not the ultimate reality. Heaven is, as Lucy says, something new and different and yet familiar: "This is still Narnia, and, more real and more beautiful than the Narnia down below" (p. 180). Once more Lewis holds the prospect out before the reader enticingly: "I can't describe it any better than that: if you ever get there, you will know what I mean" (p. 171).

The theme of longing is particularly strong at the end of the book. It grows out of the image of summer, for one thing, with its emphasis on youth ("This was his father young and merry as he could just remember him from very early days"—p. 177), and brightness ("The light ahead was growing stronger"—p. 182), and beauty ("There were forests and green slopes and sweet orchards and flashing waterfalls, one above the other, going up for ever"—p. 182). And it grows out of Lewis's usual images for longing, mountains and sensory appeals, not this time music but sweet smells: "So all of them passed in through the golden gates, into the delicious smell that blew towards them out of that garden and into the cool mixture of sunlight and shadow under the trees, walking on springy turf that was all dotted with white flowers" (p. 178). For the characters in the book, it is no longer an unsatisfied longing: they have reached their true country and will not be sent away to our world again. They are united with him they have longed for, seen now in human form: "And as He spoke He no longer looked to them like a lion" (p. 183).[9] And then things began to happen "that were so great and beautiful that I cannot write them" (pp. 183-84). Digory felt sure at the end of *The Magician's Nephew* that "they were all going to live happily ever after." But his expectation was premature: that was only the beginning of the story and much unhappiness was still to come. Now the real end of their story has arrived "and we can most truly say that they all lived happily ever after" (p. 184).

For the reader, however, the sense of longing is not satisfied but increased, by the descriptions of the new Narnia, by the review of characters from the previous books, and by the knowledge that "for us this is the end of all the stories" (p. 184). Perhaps the chief glory of the Chronicles is that the stories themselves create in many readers longings which cannot be satisfied in this world and then point readers toward the greater story in which such longings will be satisfied at last: "Now . . . they were beginning Chapter One of the Great Story, which no one on earth has read: which goes on for ever: in which every chapter is better than the one before" (p. 184).

Conclusion

THE Chronicles of Narnia are best approached, then, through their narrative art. They are, above all, stories, of interest for their plots, characters, symbols, and structural patterns. They unite the emphasis of the romance on brave knights, courteous behavior, and heroic courage with the imaginary, self-contained world of fantasy, which the reader enters and participates in temporarily for enjoyment and enlightenment, and the magical world of fairy tales and their broad, clear-cut themes contrasting good and evil. The use of myth in the Chronicles, typical of fairy tales, gives them multiple levels of meaning, aimed particularly at the imagination and the emotions; and their use of archetypal plot motifs, character types, and symbols adds depth and universality by relating them to the rest of literature and involving them in matters of ultimate concern to all people. Lewis unifies each story about a distinctive theme or tone and creates in each the flavor of a particular part of the Narnian world. All these varied elements Lewis draws into a unique and appealing combination of adventure, charm, and numinousness in plot, characters, and theme.

The Christian thought of the Chronicles, too, is best

approached through their narrative art; it is best accepted as part of the Narnian world rather than interpreted as allegory. The stories do have Christian themes, themes which go deeper than many readers, as they look for biblical parallels, suspect. And it hardly could be otherwise. Lewis claimed that he did not set out to write Christian stories, that the Christian element forced itself in of its own accord. Christianity was so deeply and fully a part of Lewis that his faith would inevitably infuse whatever he wrote. Walter Hooper called Lewis "the most thoroughly *converted* man I ever met."[1] That being the case, it was almost certain that his faith would come through as he created such elementary works as fairy tales. Perhaps without deliberately planning to, Lewis includes in the Chronicles, through images and archetypes, an overview of the faith, an indirect introduction at a children's level to the essential elements of Christianity, similar in scope and many details to *Mere Christianity*. It is one of the greatnesses of the Chronicles, however, that although they do have deeply Christian themes, they are not dependent upon Christianity. A non-Christian reader can approach the stories as fairy stories, be moved by the exciting adventures and the archetypal meanings, and not find the Christian elements obtrusive or offensive.

The Chronicles are not theological or evangelical books. There is no Narnian equivalent for the orthodox Christian belief that salvation is gained by awareness of what Christ has done and "acceptance" of him as savior. Neither Edmund, Eustace, nor Emeth, the three main examples of "salvation" in the Chronicles, knew Aslan before his conversion experience. Aslan, it is true, died in Edmund's place, but according to Susan and Lucy, Edmund did not know that at the time.

> "Does he know," whispered Lucy to Susan, "what Aslan did for him? Does he know what the arrangement with the Witch really was?"

Conclusion

"Hush! No. Of course not," said Susan.

. "Oughtn't he to be told?" said Lucy.

"Oh, surely not," said Susan. "It would be too awful for him. Think how you'd feel if you were he."

"All the same I think he ought to know," said Lucy. But at that moment they were interrupted. (*The Lion, the Witch and the Wardrobe,* pp. 177-78)

Apparently he finds out later, for he tells Eustace, after hearing how the latter was freed from his dragon skin, about Aslan, "the great Lion, the son of the Emperor over Sea, who saved me and saved Narnia" (*The Voyage of the "Dawn Treader,"* p. 92). But at the time he is saved, he knows only that Aslan is good and that he loves Aslan: "But Edmund had got past thinking about himself after all he'd been through and after the talk he'd had that morning. He just went on looking at Aslan. It didn't seem to matter what the Witch said" (*The Lion, the Witch and the Wardrobe,* p. 138).

It is much the same for Emeth, the Calormene. Always, he says, "since I was a boy, I have served Tash and my great desire was to know more of him and, if it might be, to look upon his face. But the name of Aslan was hateful to me" (*The Last Battle,* p. 162). He is admitted, however, into the new Narnia and learns there from Aslan that he has not really been a servant to Tash: "Child, all the service thou hast done to Tash, I account as service done to me" (p. 164). He knows nothing about Aslan and of course has not "accepted" Aslan when he is admitted to the new Narnia; but he loves goodness and desires truth (indeed, his name *means* Truth[2]), and these bring him into the new Narnia and lead him to love Aslan at first sight:

He was more terrible than the Flaming Mountain of Lagour, and in beauty he surpassed all that is in the world, even as the rose in bloom surpasses the dust of the desert. Then I fell at his feet and thought, Surely this is the hour of death, for the Lion (who is worthy of all honour) will know that I have

133

served Tash all my days and not him. Nevertheless, it is better to see the Lion and die than to be Tisroc of the world and live and not to have seen him. (p. 164)

And it is in terms of Emeth's love of goodness that Aslan accepts him: "Unless thy desire had been for me thou wouldst not have sought so long and so truly. For all find what they truly seek" (p. 165).

Lewis was not concerned in these books with the theology of redemption, with the steps and the means.[3] I think, therefore, that John W. Montgomery misplaces his emphasis when he writes, "The theme [unifying the Chronicles] is that basic of all themes, Redemption through Christ." He is much nearer the mark when he says later that the Chronicles can "establish in the hearts of the sensitive reader . . . a longing for the Christian story."[4] The books are, mainly, children's books, and Lewis seems to have intended that they awaken in a child a love for Aslan and for goodness which can grow, as the child matures, into love for and acceptance of Christ. The Chronicles should not be expected to influence readers to "accept" Christ, but they may lead children to love and desire Aslan and, through him, eventually, Christ.

The thesis of this book—that the Chronicles are to be read as stories, responded to with the heart before they are reflected upon with the head—is especially important when the books are read to children. In addressing authors of children's stories, Lewis argued that "We must meet children as equals in that area of our nature where we are their equals," that is, "those elements in our imagination which we share with children" ("On Three Ways of Writing for Children," *Of Other Worlds,* pp. 34, 33). Adults also, then, should read the Chronicles like children and share a child's enjoyment of the elements which appeal to the imagination. But adults, out of "interests which children would not share with us," will want to go beyond the imaginative qualities of the stories to their intellectual dimensions. The Chronicles are classics because of the way the intellectual reinforces the imaginative, and there is value for adults in seeing and discussing both aspects together; for them, and for children increasingly as they grow older, a response with the head can and should follow a response of the heart. But to explicate the "meanings" of the books to children would be, in Lewis's words, "patronizing" (*Of Other Worlds,* p. 34), talking down to them out of superior adult interests and perspectives. The Chronicles are not allegories needing interpretation for full effect: they are stories to be enjoyed. Children should be left to enjoy them, imaginatively and emotionally, without being asked to reflect upon their "significance." And because of the archetypal nature of the stories, because their roots reach down to basic human instincts and emotions, out of that enjoyment "meaning" will come, at its own time and in its own way.

Notes

Introduction

1. Walter Hooper, "C. S. Lewis," *The Franciscan,* 9 (September 1967), 173.

2. C. Hugh Holman, *A Handbook to Literature,* 3rd ed. (New York: Odyssey, 1972), p. 13.

3. "On Stories," in *Of Other Worlds: Essays and Stories,* ed. Walter Hooper (London: Bles, 1966), p. 19.

4. "Psycho-Analysis and Literary Criticism," in *Selected Literary Essays,* ed. Walter Hooper (Cambridge: Cambridge University Press, 1969), p. 286.

5. See Lewis's Preface to *Mere Christianity,* pp. 5-6. The radio talks, delivered on the BBC in 1941, 1942, and 1944, were published in three volumes: *Broadcast Talks* [in America *The Case for Christianity*] (London: Bles, 1942); *Christian Behaviour* (London: Bles, 1943); *Beyond Personality* (London: Bles, 1944).

6. As for example, this use of the Bible by Kathryn A. Lindskoog in commenting on the adventures of Shasta in *The Horse and His Boy:* "Aslan deals with each individual in a unique way to bring him to the same place. But he does not give an account of his relationship with any one person to any other person. When asked, he always answers, 'I am telling you your story, not hers. I tell no-one any story but his own.' As Christ said when asked 'What about this man?', '... what is that to you? Follow me!' (John 21:22, RSV)"—*The Lion of Judah in Never-Never Land* (Grand Rapids: Eerdmans, 1973), pp. 65-66.

Reading with the Heart

Chapter 1—*Reading with the Heart*

1. *A Preface to Paradise Lost* (London: Oxford University Press, 1942), p. 1.
2. See especially *Of Other Worlds,* pp. 24-28, 36-37.
3. Lee T. Lemon, *A Glossary for the Study of English* (New York: Oxford University Press, 1971), p. 4.
4. J. R. R. Tolkien, "On Fairy-Stories," in *Essays Presented to Charles Williams* (London: Oxford University Press, 1947), p. 43. Lewis cites this essay approvingly in "On Three Ways of Writing for Children," in *Of Other Worlds,* pp. 26-27.
5. Tolkien, "On Fairy-Stories," pp. 43, 71.
6. Holman, *A Handbook to Literature,* p. 219.
7. Tolkien, "On Fairy-Stories," p. 60.
8. George MacDonald, "The Fantastic Imagination," in *A Dish of Orts: Chiefly Papers on the Imagination, and on Shakespere,* Enlarged Edition (London: Sampson Low Marston and Company, 1893), p. 314. Thus the spell in *The Voyage of the "Dawn Treader"* is broken momentarily when Lewis forgets his rule about invisibility. Spears in the hands of the Dufflepuds are invisible—"They get visible when they leave us" (p. 120). Three pages later, however, plates and dishes in their hands are not invisible: "It was very funny to see the plates and dishes coming to the table and not to see anyone carrying them" (p. 123).
9. Charles A. Brady, "Finding God in Narnia," *America,* 27 October 1956, p. 104.
10. John W. Montgomery, "The Chronicles of Narnia and the Adolescent Reader," *Journal of Religious Education,* 54 (September-October 1959), 423 [reprinted in *Myth, Allegory and Gospel,* ed. John W. Montgomery (Minneapolis: Bethany Fellowship, 1974)]. Similarly, M. S. Crouch, "The Chronicles of Narnia," *The Junior Bookshelf,* 20 (November 1956), 246.
11. MacDonald, "The Fantastic Imagination," p. 317.
12. See *An Experiment in Criticism* (Cambridge: Cambridge University Press, 1961), pp. 41-44 and *Miracles* (London: Bles, 1947), p. 161n [Ch. 15].
13. Preface to *The Pilgrim's Regress,* 3rd ed. (London: Bles, 1943), p. 13.
14. *Letters of C. S. Lewis,* ed. W. H. Lewis (London: Bles, 1966), p. 283.
15. MacDonald, "The Fantastic Imagination," pp. 321-22.
16. I have found the writings of Leland Ryken on archetypal criticism very helpful. See especially the third chapter of his forthcoming book, *Triumphs of the Imagination: Literature in Christian Perspective* (Downers Grove, Ill.: InterVarsity Press).
17. Northrop Frye, *Anatomy of Criticism, Four Essays* (Princeton: Princeton University Press, 1957), p. 99. Lewis often

gives attention to archetypes in his own criticism, especially in *A Preface to Paradise Lost* and *Spenser's Images of Life,* ed. Alastair Fowler (Cambridge: Cambridge University Press, 1967).

18. Northrop Frye, *Fables of Identity: Studies in Poetic Mythology* (New York: Harcourt, Brace and World, 1963), p. 15; *The Educated Imagination* (Bloomington: Indiana University Press, 1964), p. 55. One scholar suggests that the monomyth is "the center of reality as perceived by creative man in all ages and nations and under a number of forms of expression—ritual, myth, scripture, dream, even history. . . . There is little doubt that the myth pattern does embody, in a simple and usable form, a principle of reality so vast as to have implications for nearly every area of life"—Charles Moorman, *A Knyght There Was: The Evolution of the Knight in Literature* (Lexington: University of Kentucky Press, 1967), p. 33. Frye sees the identity theme as more inclusive than, even as encompassing, the two other well-known versions of the "monomyth," that of the earth mother, as proposed by Robert Graves— *The White Goddess: A Historical Grammar of Poetic Myth* (London: Faber and Faber, 1948)—and that of the hero, as advocated by Joseph Campbell in *The Hero with a Thousand Faces,* Bollingen Series XVII (Princeton: Princeton University Press, 1949). Frye's literary approach to archetypes would also, I think, be more acceptable to Lewis than the more psychological approaches of Graves and Campbell.

19. See "Myth Became Fact," in *God in the Dock: Essays on Theology and Ethics,* ed. Walter Hooper (Grand Rapids: Eerdmans, 1970), pp. 66-67. Lewis mentions in several places his belief that God used the myths of the pagans as a prefiguring of or preparation for Christianity—see especially "Religion without Dogma?" in *God in the Dock,* p. 132, and *Surprised by Joy: The Shape of My Early Life* (London: Bles, 1955), pp. 64-65, 221-22 [Chs. 4, 15]. Archetypes, then, as the building blocks out of which myths are constructed, are very important because they may have been implanted within us by God: Lewis speculates, in commenting on Jung's theories about a universal subconscious, that "the mystery of primordial images is deeper, their origin more remote, their cave more hid, their fountain less accessible than those suspect who have yet dug deepest" ("Psycho-Analysis and Literary Criticism," in *Selected Literary Essays,* p. 300).

20. Thus the index prepared for the book in the Marion E. Wade Collection at Wheaton College includes an entry for "Satan" which lists the various appearances of the White Witch.

21. According to Jewish legend, Lilith was the first wife of Adam, created with him from the dust of the earth. As Adam's apparent coequal, Lilith refused to be subordinate and obedient to Adam or to bear children for him. Eventually she ran away

and became the enemy and oppressor of men, children, and women who accept their "proper" role. For a good summary, see Glen GoodKnight, "Lilith in Narnia," in *Narnia Conference Proceedings* (Maywood, Calif.: The Mythopoeic Society, 1970), pp. 15-19.

22. In *The Lion, the Witch and the Wardrobe* Aslan attacks the Witch on page 174; page 175 says specifically that the Witch is dead. In *Prince Caspian,* on the other hand, the Hag argues she is still alive—not, however, because she is the Devil but because she is a witch: "Who ever heard of a witch that really died? You can always get them back" (p. 165). The account of the Witch in *The Magician's Nephew* (where her origin in Charn does not mention Lilithian ancestry and where she is said to have gained immortality by eating one of the silver apples) does not correspond with the details in *The Lion, the Witch and the Wardrobe.*

23. From an unpublished letter to Mr. Kinter, 30 July 1954, now in the Bodleian Library, Oxford. I am grateful to the trustees of the estate of C. S. Lewis for permission to quote from this letter.

24. Some readers of the Chronicles have objected to the inclusion of Father Christmas in the story. Roger Lancelyn Green, for example, urged Lewis to omit him as somehow "breaking the magic for a moment: he still does not seem to fit quite comfortably into his place" (Roger Lancelyn Green and Walter Hooper, *C. S. Lewis: A Biography* [London: Collins, 1974], p. 241; similarly, Clyde S. Kilby, *The Christian World of C. S. Lewis* [Grand Rapids: Eerdmans, 1964], p. 145). The inclusion of Christmas itself, however, would seem to be the more basic inconsistency. Christmas celebrates the birth of Christ in his earthly incarnation. To be true to his fantasy world, Lewis should perhaps have created a Narnian equivalent to our Christmas instead of taking it into Narnia.

25. M. H. Abrams, *A Glossary of Literary Terms,* 3rd ed. (New York: Holt, Rinehart and Winston, 1971), p. 22, and Holman, *A Handbook to Literature,* p. 309.

26. John Alexander, "What is Narnia Teaching My Kids?", *The Other Side,* July 1977, pp. 38-42.

Chapter 2—*"A Great Sculptor's Shop"*

1. "It All Began with a Picture . . . ," in *Of Other Worlds,* p. 42. See also *Of Other Worlds,* pp. 32 and 36. A useful, authoritative account of the composition and publication of the Chronicles can be found in Green and Hooper, *C. S. Lewis: A Biography,* pp. 236-56.

Notes

2. *English Literature in the Sixteenth Century, Excluding Drama,* Volume III of the *Oxford History of English Literature,* ed. F. P. Wilson and Bonamy Dobrée (Oxford: Clarendon Press, 1954), p. 8.

3. Tolkien, "On Fairy-Stories," pp. 70-71.

4. *Out of the Silent Planet* (London: John Lane, 1938), p. 157 [Ch. 20].

5. *That Hideous Strength: A Modern Fairy-Tale for Grown-Ups* (London: John Lane, 1945), p. 177 [Ch. 7].

6. *The Abolition of Man* (New York: Macmillan, 1947), p. 12.

7. "The Poison of Subjectivism," in *Christian Reflections,* ed. Walter Hooper (Grand Rapids: Eerdmans, 1967), p. 75.

8. *Ibid.,* p. 73.

Chapter 3—*"Finding Out by Experience"*

1. "Note" added to the American edition of *Till We Have Faces: A Myth Retold* (1956; New York: Harcourt, Brace and Company, 1957), p. 313.

2. Edith Hamilton, *Mythology* (Boston: Little, Brown and Company, 1942), pp. 73-74.

Chapter 4—*"Putting the Clock Back"*

1. For several details in this paragraph, see Howard R. Patch, *The Other World* (Cambridge, Mass.: Harvard University Press, 1950).

2. Cf. also, "We are like eggs at present. And you cannot go on indefinitely being just an ordinary, decent egg. We must be hatched or go bad" (*Mere Christianity,* p. 169).

3. Lewis made the same point in his first prose work, *The Pilgrim's Regress* (London: J. M. Dent, 1933). The title is a play on *The Pilgrim's Progress* by John Bunyan (1678). Achievement of Bunyan's spiritual "progress," Lewis is suggesting, first requires a "regress," doing an about turn and returning to the right road.

4. See *The Lion, the Witch and the Wardrobe,* pp. 102-3, and *Prince Caspian,* pp. 152-54, 192-98, and 205-6, respectively.

5. There are also myths about round worlds in Narnia (*The Voyage of the "Dawn Treader,"* p. 201) and, before the appearance of the four children, myths about humans (*The Lion, the Witch and the Wardrobe,* p. 12).

6. Further confirmation that the story Lucy read in the Magician's Book is the story of Christ is the similarity of this line to the concluding lines of Chapter 10, where Aslan says to Lucy about the story, "I will tell it to you for years and years."

7. *Surprised by Joy,* pp. 23-24 [Ch. 1]. Longing in the Chronicles is discussed at greater length in an essay by Eliane Tixier, "Imagination Baptized, or, 'Holiness' in the Chronicles of Narnia," in *The Longing for a Form: Essays on the Fiction of C. S. Lewis,* ed. Peter J. Schakel (Kent, Ohio: The Kent State University Press, 1977), pp. 136-58. The fullest discussion of Longing, or *Sehnsucht,* is by Corbin Scott Carnell, *Bright Shadow of Reality: C. S. Lewis and the Feeling Intellect* (Grand Rapids: Eerdmans, 1974).

8. "Is Progress Possible?", in *God in the Dock,* pp. 311-16.

Chapter 5—*"You Must Use the Map"*

1. Northrop Frye, *The Secular Scripture: A Study of the Structure of Romance* (Cambridge, Mass.: Harvard University Press, 1976), p. 97.

2. See also p. 200. In a paper suggesting several sources for *The Silver Chair* and relating them to the theme of knowledge, John D. Cox finds an important antecedent for the Witch in Edmund Spenser's *The Faerie Queene* ("Epistemological Release in *The Silver Chair*," in *The Longing for a Form,* pp. 161-62).

3. See *The Lion, the Witch and the Wardrobe,* p. 77, and *The Magician's Nephew,* pp. 100-1 and 174-75.

Chapter 6—*"Throwing Up the Sponge"*

1. *"The Weight of Glory" and Other Addresses* (New York: Macmillan, 1949), p. 4.

2. *Surprised By Joy,* pp. 74-75 [Ch. 5].

Chapter 7—*"Putting the Human Machine Right"*

1. Adapted from Leland Ryken, *The Literature of the Bible* (Grand Rapids: Zondervan, 1974), p. 23.

2. Lewis seems to have had in mind intemperate curiosity of the type discussed by Howard Schultz in *Milton and Forbidden*

Knowledge (New York: Modern Language Association of America, 1955), pp. 1-10. Digory was "wild with curiosity" (p. 49) and apparently he should have realized that his desire to ring the bell was wrong. There would seem, however, to be a very thin line dividing such irresponsible inquisitiveness from Reepicheep's desire to enter the blackness surrounding the Dark Island. I cannot help thinking that if Reepicheep had come upon the golden bell in *The Voyage of the "Dawn Treader,"* he would have said, and seemed right in saying, "Here is as great an adventure as ever I heard of, and here, if we turn back, no little impeachment of all our honours" (p. 152).

3. In one of the most interesting sections of his essay "C. S. Lewis's Narnia and the 'Grand Design' " (in *The Longing for a Form,* pp. 119-35), Charles A. Huttar compares Lewis's creation story to the accounts in Genesis, *Paradise Lost,* Lucretius, and Ovid.

4. The lion's song also reflects the biblical idea of creation by the Word (see John 1:1-3).

5. The "Outline of Narnian history" was drawn up by Lewis after he completed the seven stories. He gave it in manuscript form to Walter Hooper, who has included it in his essay, "Past Watchful Dragons: The Fairy Tales of C. S. Lewis," a valuable and informative essay on the composition and meaning of the Chronicles—in *Imagination and the Spirit: Essays in Literature and the Christian Faith Presented to Clyde S. Kilby,* ed. Charles A. Huttar (Grand Rapids: Eerdmans, 1971), pp. 298-301.

6. There is some debate over the "correct" order for reading the Chronicles. Some readers of Lewis prefer that *The Magician's Nephew* be read before *The Lion, the Witch and the Wardrobe,* so that the reader may become familiar with the origins of Narnia and of the wardrobe. Clyde S. Kilby treats them in that order in *The Christian World of C. S. Lewis,* p. 117, and Anne Arnott suggests it in *The Secret Country of C. S. Lewis* (Grand Rapids: Eerdmans, 1975), p. 125. Lewis himself gave qualified approval to it in an unpublished letter (to Laurence Krieg, 22 April 1957). The only reason for reading *The Magician's Nephew* first, however, is for the chronological sequence of events, and that, as every storyteller knows, is quite unimportant as a reason. Often the early events in a sequence have a greater impact or effect as a flashback, told after later events which provide background and establish perspective. So it is, I believe, with the Chronicles. The artistry, the archetypes, and the pattern of Christian thought all make it preferable to read the books in the order of their publication.

Several artistic effects in *The Lion, the Witch and the Wardrobe* are undercut when one of the other books is read before it.

Reading with the Heart

The careful use of details to enable readers to share Lucy's initial experience in Narnia and the equally careful buildup before Aslan's name is mentioned work best and have their fullest impact if this book is one's introduction to Narnia. The first reference to Aslan is by Mr. Beaver, when he meets the children in the woods: "They say Aslan is on the move—perhaps has already landed." The passage, significantly, assumes that readers have not already read other books about Narnia: "And now a very curious thing happened. None of the children knew who Aslan was any more than you do; but the moment the Beaver had spoken these words everyone felt quite different" (p. 64). Of course no other books were written—or even planned, apparently—when these words were written. But the fact that other books came later, filling in previous events, does not alter the artistry of the first book.

The introduction to the lion is not at all the same, artistically or emotionally, in *The Magician's Nephew:* it assumes, on the contrary, that readers do have prior knowledge of him. When the voice first begins to sing on page 98, Lewis emphasizes the beauty, not the mysteriousness, of it. And when the sun rises and the singer becomes visible, the story says simply, "It was a Lion. Huge, shaggy, and bright it stood facing the risen sun" (p. 102). There is no buildup like "Don't you know who is the King of Beasts? Aslan is a lion—*the* Lion, the great Lion" and no introduction to him as "the son of the great Emperor-Beyond-the-Sea" as there is in *The Lion, the Witch and the Wardrobe* (p. 75); the narrator seems to assume that readers already know who the lion is. Indeed, Lewis never does bother to identify him until the animals, as soon as they are given the gift of speech, say his name—they simply know it. Artistically, then, *The Magician's Nephew* fits in better as a flashback, filling in the background of places and people already known, than as a first book introducing those places and people.

The archetypal pattern of *The Magician's Nephew* also fits better as sixth than as first in the series. *The Magician's Nephew* and *The Last Battle* together depict through interlocking images a complete seasonal cycle which mirrors the full cycle of Narnian history. The autumn/spring story of *The Magician's Nephew* complements the winter/summer story of *The Last Battle;* the symbolism reinforces the plot detail in unifying the beginning of Narnia with the end. This archetypal pattern is most effective if *The Magician's Nephew* and *The Last Battle* are read together: the immediate juxtaposition of the two books brings out well the completeness and unity of Narnian history. And that completeness, the point that the Narnian world has a beginning and an ending, along with a creator who existed before the beginning and will continue to exist after the ending, is a central part of the meaning of the stories, a part that is more easily missed if five other books separate *The Magician's Nephew* from *The Last Battle*.

Finally, the order in which the Christian ideas are presented is most effective if the Chronicles are read in the order of publication. The situation is parallel to that of *Mere Christianity*. The discussion of "Christian Behaviour" could not have the same meaning it has now if it were the opening section of *Mere Christianity*. Coming as it does after the sections on "Right and Wrong as a Clue to the Meaning of the Universe" and "What Christians Believe," it grows out of the premises about law, grace, and faith laid out in the earlier sections. So it is, in a less tightly logical way, for the Chronicles of Narnia. When *The Magician's Nephew* is read first, the theme of morality loses the context the earlier books established. The themes of law, faith, growth, and divine guidance and care in the earlier books provide a Christian basis for the moral instruction; the morality grows out of faith, not just out of a desire to "do better."

Chapter 8—*"My True Country"*

1. "Is Progress Possible?", in *God in the Dock,* p. 314.
2. *Ibid.,* p. 313.
3. "Cross-Examination," in *God in the Dock,* p. 265.
4. "Christian Apologetics," in *God in the Dock,* p. 89.
5. Although Lewis's judgment scene resembles that of Matthew 25, it may have had another source as well. Professor Kirke says, late in the book, "It's all in Plato, all in Plato" (p. 170), and the judgment scene, at least, is in Plato. In the *Phaedo* (113) Plato writes that "when the dead come to the place whither the spirit conveys each, first the judges divide them into those who have lived well and piously, and those who have not." And in *The Republic* (Book X) the judges, as they divided the dead, "gave judgment, and, according to the judgment, they commanded the just men to proceed to the right and upwards through heaven . . . ; the unjust they sent down to the left." See *Great Dialogues of Plato,* trans. W. H. D. Rouse, ed. Eric Warmington and Philip G. Rouse (New York: The New American Library, 1956), pp. 517 and 415. The parallels to Plato were first pointed out by Nathan C. Starr in a paper, "Eschatology in C. S. Lewis's *The Last Battle,*" presented at the convention of the Modern Language Association of America, December, 1975.
6. Jadis's description of the fall of Charnian civilization in *The Magician's Nephew* is a story of autumn—the ultimate dis-

solution of that world occurs while the children are in Narnia and is not actually a part of the story. *The Last Battle* goes further, to depict the total destruction of the Narnian world, thus a story of winter.

7. *The Last Battle* has been compared to the prophecies regarding the end times in the Bible. "In *The Last Battle* the Biblical story of the end of human history is graphically portrayed: the Antichrist, the battle of Armegeddon, death . . . , the General Resurrection, and the consummation of the Plan of Redemption in a New Heaven and a New Earth" (Montgomery, "The Chronicles of Narnia and the Adolescent Reader," p. 424). *The Last Battle* is an apocalyptic story, one that deals with end times, and that, even without Lewis's familiarity with the Bible, would give it resemblances to the biblical account. The story draws upon Matthew 24 and 25, with their warnings of false Christs who will deceive many, false prophets, war and tribulation, the darkening of the sun, moon, and stars, the coming of Christ, and the final judgment. But there is no Antichrist figure in *The Last Battle:* Shift is not powerful enough and Tash does not lead the opposition to Aslan or participate as leader of the evil forces in the final battle. Tash is opposite to Aslan (p. 165) but he does not oppose Aslan: the Calormenes invade Narnia out of their own selfish desires, not at Tash's urgings. *The Last Battle,* one should conclude, does not portray the end of human history: it portrays the end of Narnian history. It speaks to our world, as any apocalyptic myth does; but to look for parallels and allegories is to raise the wrong questions about it. (See Walter Hooper, "Narnia: The Author, the Critics, and the Tale," in *The Longing for a Form,* pp. 113-18.)

8. Tash does not seem to be the Devil, but a pagan god, like Baal in the Old Testament or Ungit in *Till We Have Faces.* The worship of Tash, therefore, includes what Lewis in his essay "Religion without Dogma?" calls "the obscenities and cruelties of paganism" (*God in the Dock,* p. 143). In our world such gods are not real, and even in Narnia the Lamb says, "I don't believe there's any such person as Tash" (p. 31). But in Narnia other mythical figures have turned out to be real, and so does Tash (pp. 81-83).

9. Hooper, "Narnia: The Author, the Critics, and the Tale," pp. 117-18.

Conclusion

1. Walter Hooper, Preface to *God in the Dock,* p. 12.

2. In a footnote to *The Abolition of Man,* Lewis mentions that the Hebrew word *emeth* means "truth" or "faithfulness": "*Emeth*

is that which does not deceive, does not 'give,' does not change, that which holds water" (pp. 11-12n).

3. Work on this book was completed before publication of Gilbert Meilaender's fine study *The Taste for the Other: The Social and Ethical Thought of C. S. Lewis* (Grand Rapids: Eerdmans, 1978), so that I was not able to profit from his consideration of Lewis's views of faith and grace on pages 36-38. He shows that the lack of emphasis on the means of salvation is consistent with Lewis's Anglo-Catholic theology: "It is the vision of God, not justification by faith, which is the cornerstone of his theological system" (p. 38). Meilaender's discussion of "pilgrimage" and morality also covers in a valuable way themes examined in this book.

4. Montgomery, "The Chronicles of Narnia and the Adolescent Reader," pp. 423, 427.

Table for Converting Page References to Chapter Numbers

To locate quotations in other editions of the Chronicles of Narnia and *Mere Christianity*, use the page numbers below (from the Macmillan paperback editions) to identify the chapter and the approximate location in the chapter of passages cited by page number in the text.

The Lion, the Witch and the Wardrobe

Pp. 1-8: Ch. 1

Pp. 9-19: Ch. 2

Pp. 20-28: Ch. 3

Pp. 29-39: Ch. 4

Pp. 40-49: Ch. 5

Pp. 50-59: Ch. 6

Pp. 60-71: Ch. 7

Pp. 72-83: Ch. 8

Pp. 84-94: Ch. 9

Pp. 95-106: Ch. 10

Pp. 107-118: Ch. 11

Pp. 119-129: Ch. 12

Pp. 130-141: Ch. 13

Pp. 142-152: Ch. 14

Pp. 153-163: Ch. 15

Pp. 164-174: Ch. 16

Pp. 175-186: Ch. 17

Prince Caspian

Pp. 1-11: Ch. 1

Pp. 12-25: Ch. 2

Pp. 26-36: Ch. 3

Pp. 37-51: Ch. 4

Pp. 52-67: Ch. 5

Pp. 68-78: Ch. 6

Pp. 79-93: Ch. 7

Pp. 94-108: Ch. 8

Pp. 109-124: Ch. 9

Pp. 125-140: Ch. 10

Pp. 141-154: Ch. 11

Pp. 155-169: Ch. 12

Pp. 170-182: Ch. 13

Pp. 183-198: Ch. 14

Pp. 199-216: Ch. 15

The Voyage of the "Dawn Treader"

The Silver Chair

The Horse and His Boy

Table for Converting Page References

The Magician's Nephew

Pp. 1-14: Ch. 1
Pp. 15-27: Ch. 2
Pp. 28-40: Ch. 3
Pp. 41-53: Ch. 4
Pp. 54-65: Ch. 5
Pp. 66-78: Ch. 6
Pp. 79-91: Ch. 7
Pp. 92-103: Ch. 8

Pp. 104-116: Ch. 9
Pp. 117-128: Ch. 10
Pp. 129-140: Ch. 11
Pp. 141-153: Ch. 12
Pp. 154-165: Ch. 13
Pp. 166-176: Ch. 14
Pp. 177-186: Ch. 15

The Last Battle

Pp. 1-11: Ch. 1
Pp. 12-22: Ch. 2
Pp. 23-33: Ch. 3
Pp. 34-44: Ch. 4
Pp. 45-55: Ch. 5
Pp. 56-67: Ch. 6
Pp. 68-80: Ch. 7
Pp. 81-91: Ch. 8

Pp. 92-102: Ch. 9
Pp. 103-113: Ch. 10
Pp. 114-124: Ch. 11
Pp. 125-135: Ch. 12
Pp. 136-148: Ch. 13
Pp. 149-160: Ch. 14
Pp. 161-171: Ch. 15
Pp. 172-184: Ch. 16

Mere Christianity

Pp. 17-21: Bk. I, Ch. 1
Pp. 21-26: Bk. I, Ch. 2
Pp. 26-30: Bk. I, Ch. 3
Pp. 31-35: Bk. I, Ch. 4
Pp. 36-39: Bk. I, Ch. 5
Pp. 43-46: Bk. II, Ch. 1
Pp. 46-51: Bk. II, Ch. 2
Pp. 51-56: Bk. II, Ch. 3
Pp. 56-61: Bk. II, Ch. 4

Pp. 62-66: Bk. II, Ch. 5
Pp. 69-73: Bk. III, Ch. 1
Pp. 74-78: Bk. III, Ch. 2
Pp. 78-83: Bk. III, Ch. 3
Pp. 83-87: Bk. III, Ch. 4
Pp. 88-95: Bk. III, Ch. 5
Pp. 95-103: Bk. III, Ch. 6
Pp. 104-108: Bk. III, Ch. 7
Pp. 108-114: Bk. III, Ch. 8

Reading with the Heart

INDEX

(Unlabeled titles are by Lewis)